Woman's Place
Is at the Typewriter

Class and Culture

A series edited by Bruce Laurie
and Milton Cantor

Woman's Place Is at the Typewriter

Office Work and Office Workers
1870–1930

Margery W. Davies

Temple University Press / Philadelphia

Temple University Press, Philadelphia 19122
© 1982 by Temple University. All rights reserved
Published 1982
Printed in the United States of America

Library of Congress Cataloging in Publication Data

Davies, Margery W.
  Woman's place is at the typewriter.

  (Class and culture)
  Revision of thesis (Ph.D.)—Brandeis University.
  Includes index.
  1. Women—Employment—United States—History.   2. Clerks—
United States—History.   3. Sex role in the work environment—
United States—History.   I. Title.   II. Series.
HD6095.D37   1982   305.4'3651   82-13694
ISBN 0-87722-291-6

For Arthur

Contents

Contents

viii

Preface

In the process of working on this book, I have accrued debts to a number of people. I first began investigating the topic as a research assistant for a project on labor market segmentation headed by Michael Reich, Richard C. Edwards and David M. Gordon. Their ideas and criticisms helped to launch my study of the feminization of clerical work, which was later to become the subject of my doctoral dissertation at Brandeis University. My thesis advisors, Egon Bittner, George Ross, and Charlotte Weissberg, pushed me to sort out the threads of my argument and provided numerous valuable insights about major and minor points.

Every writer should be fortunate enough to have editors like Bruce Laurie and Milton Cantor. They had not only the patience to slog through my dissertation, but also the generosity to give me page-by-page suggestions about how to revise it. They then took this revised manuscript and went over it with a fine-toothed comb, helping me to improve the style and to sharpen my argument. I am happy to take full responsibility for the basic thesis of this book. To the extent that my ideas emerge with any clarity, however, the credit must be shared by these two editors. I am also indebted to my copy editor, Patrick O'Kane, who did an excellent job of catching my careless mistakes and improving my use of the English language; and to Jim O'Brien, who did the index.

Both Linda Gordon and Allen Hunter have been very generous with their time: helping me to clear up my thinking on substantive points when I found myself confused; giving me healthy doses of moral support; and giving me time by helping to take care of my children. Molly Fontaine ran baby and toddler playgroups that included three of my children over the years. Without the time and peace of mind that this afforded me, I would have had much more difficulty finishing this book.

My most important ally in my efforts to combine parenthood, political activity and academic work has been my husband, Arthur MacEwan. As well as giving me unflagging emotional support, he has helped me with both the content and oganization of the book. While we are both committed to creating a state of affairs where husbands are thanked as frequently as wives on the acknowledgments page, I am very glad that I have a husband whose actions match his beliefs.

Woman's Place
Is at the Typewriter

1

Introduction

Several years ago a friend of mine, who was teaching at a university wealthy enough to provide its professors with private secretaries, hired a man as his secretary. Although it would be going too far to say that this created a sensation, the situation helped expose the popular assumption that secretaries were women. Often someone would come into the office and ask Jim if he or she could speak to the secretary. "I *am* the secretary," Jim was forced to reply. After a while he got fed up with this and started responding with "I can help you. What can I do for you?" This at times resulted in the visitor's insisting on talking to the secretary, and Jim's insisting that he could help. My friend found himself more uncomfortable asking Jim to do things than he had been with the previous secretary, who was a woman. For his part, Jim did not regard his office job as his main occupation; his greater interest was acting in amateur theater. It would be safe to say that everyone, Jim included, thought his job a little odd for a man. This is quite a testimony to the strength of popular beliefs about men's and women's work, particularly since little over a century ago, *all* office workers were men.

In most societies people assume that women and men have proper places. This sexual division of labor is usually seen as natural. Thus in the United States today it seems proper that woman's place is at the stove, or with the children, or in the elementary school classroom, or at the typewriter. Moreover, it

3

seems natural not only that such chores are gender-specific today, but also that they were always so.

These beliefs ought to be scrutinized most carefully. Sexual stereotyping, after all, plays a substantial role in limiting any female or male to those activities deemed appropriate to her or his sex. Thus, when an occupation has shifted from one sex to another, it merits attention, since the shift stands as concrete illustration that the sexual division of labor is neither universal nor unchanging. I hope that this book proves useful to the clerical worker who asks why the office hierarchy has women at the bottom and men at the top. If her employer's answer is that "woman's place is at the typewriter" and that it has always been that way, at the very least she will know that that is not true, whether or not she can get her boss to believe it.

Occupational sex segregation is often accompanied by sex discrimination. Women and men are *not* separate but equal in the labor force. Women's work tends to be lower paid and less prestigious than men's. The history and dynamics of discrimination must be probed: understanding the obstacles is an essential first step in bringing about change.

Woman's place at the typewriter must be explored within a dual structure that takes into account patriarchal social relations and such political-economic forces as the expansion of capitalist firms and the increased demand for clerical labor. Patriarchy and political economy may be separated for analytic purposes, but this does not mean that they operate independently. On the contrary, the particular forms that patriarchy has taken in the United States have been influenced by the stages of capitalist development, just as American capitalism partly owes its particular form to patriarchal relations. Nevertheless, the distinction is useful in explaining certain developments. The issue is not whether any given phenomenon can be completely attributed either to patriarchy or to political-economic forces. The issue rather is how "woman's place" is determined by the interaction between them.

In discussing the feminization of clerical workers and

changes in the organization of clerical work, this book spans the late nineteenth century and the first three decades of the twentieth. During this period, the class position of office workers changed perceptibly. The typical clerk in the early nineteenth-century office was an aspiring businessman, apprenticed to the petite bourgeoisie or the capitalist class. By 1930 office workers were no longer apprentice capitalists. Some might be promoted to lower-level managerial positions such as supervisor of a typing pool or head of the bookkeeping department; most, however, were likely to remain clerical workers all of their working lives. The enormous expansion of clerical jobs that started in the late nineteenth century, the changing composition of the labor force, and the proletarianization of clerical employees transformed autonomous male clerks into female office operatives and members of the working class. While this shift has only recently been acknowledged and the membership of clerical workers in the working class become less a matter of dispute, the change had basically taken place by 1930.

This shift in class position, it goes without saying, is inextricably bound up with changes in the organization of clerical work. Prior to the late nineteenth century, clerical workers performed a wide variety of tasks. They were often jacks-of-all-trades in offices that were quite small by twentieth-century standards, and thus they "learned the business." By 1930, however, clerical workers could be divided into two basic groups: lower-level employees who executed a small number of routine tasks in a manner that was increasingly controlled and prescribed by employers; and those on a higher level, best typified by private secretaries, who were responsible for a wide variety of tasks. This latter group was encouraged to exercise considerable initiative and enjoyed some independence in their work. But despite their greater knowledge, independence, and control, private secretaries remained unambiguously subordinate to their employers. By 1930, then, there was indeed a secretarial proletariat.

These, in sum, are the major themes of this book. Woman's place at the typewriter is historically specific rather than ordained by nature; the feminization of clerical work reflects the interaction between patriarchal social relations and political-economic forces; and the working-class status of contemporoay office workers is rooted in changes in the organization of clerical work that began at the end of the nineteenth century.

The historical evidence is somewhat piecemeal because the changes in clerical work often were subtle and slow enough to go more or less unnoticed. Furthermore, clerical workers up to 1930 were relatively quiescent. Business histories and internal corporation records, where one would expect to find abundant information about changes in the nature of clerical work, tend to concentrate on such matters as techniques of capital accumulation, the personal struggles and weaknesses of individual managers, and technological developments. Those business histories that do contain information about clerical workers are a good source, since they describe situations in actual firms. The authors, however, are almost always court biographers, whose allegiance to the firm biases their stories, and this must be taken into account. Furthermore, the history of one firm is not necessarily typical of all firms. With these caveats in mind, it is possible to use business histories to great advantage.

There do not exist for office workers the newspaper accounts of strikes, union records, or governmental investigations that have been the source of much material about industrial workers, since before 1930, clerical workers rarely joined unions, much less went on strike. Still, there are many sources that shed light on clerical work and workers. These fall into two categories: descriptions of an office or a typical work day; and advice to clerical workers about how to do their jobs well, the treatment they can expect, or how to get promoted. Although these articles provide only sporadic evidence at best, and must be read as one writer's view of a situation rather than as reflections of general opinion, they provide many useful insights.

Commentary that derives from the campaign to apply principles of scientific management to the office is the one truly coherent body of literature about clerical work and workers. Such writings are found in a few books and in *Industrial Management* and *System* (later to become *Business Week*), two magazines interested in promoting scientific office management. They contain a wealth of information, especially in comparison to the scantiness of other sources.

Novels and short stories describing clerical workers and office work are also useful. Evidence from such sources must be used carefully, being the product of the writer's imagination and possibly designed to serve artistic ends rather than to depict real life accurately. Nevertheless, no writer is totally divorced from his or her social context, and fictional accounts of offices and clerical workers do reflect actual experiences to some extent. Although it would be a mistake to allow the burden of proof to rest on these stories, they are social artifacts and can be used to fill in the picture.

One may wonder whether the analysis of clerical work and workers found in this book has contemporary relevance, for there are indications that fundamental changes are at present occurring in the organization of office work. The introduction of the computer and automation into the offices of the 1950s and 1960s did not, at first, produce significant changes. These technological advances were, however, the prelude to changes that are likely to result in some basic restructuring of the workplace. Witness, for instance, the storage of information on computer disks and tapes, the retrieval of that information in purely electronic form, and the consequent elimination of paper as a medium for storing information. A significant reduction in the amount of paper used by an office could well mean severe cutbacks in the numbers of file clerks and typists employed. Then, too, there is the effort to reduce the number of private secretaries and typists through the introduction of word-processing centers. Fundamental and far-reaching though such changes may be with respect to the organization of clerical work, however, they are still only at an early stage. It is safe to say that the basic outlines of the organization of office work that were visible in 1930 still hold today.

2

The Office

before the Civil War

One comes away from a visit to the offices of a skyscraper with the image of large, well-lighted rooms where female clerical workers preside over metal desks and filing cabinets, copying machines, typewriters, and large potted plants. But little more than a hundred years ago, the picture was very different. Offices were small and staffed by men. In "Bartleby," Herman Melville describes the clerks in a Wall Street lawyer's office. Turkey, an Englishman of sixty, always drank a good deal with his noontime dinner and his florid face thereafter "blazed like a grate full of Christmas coals." It was also in the afternoon that Turkey's "business capacities [were] seriously disturbed for the remainder of the twenty-four hours. Not that he was absolutely idle, or averse to business, then; far from it. The difficulty was, he was apt to be altogether too energetic. There was a strange, inflamed, flurried, flighty recklessness of activity about him. He would be incautious in dipping his pen into his inkstand. All his blots upon my documents, were dropped there after twelve o'clock, meridian. Indeed, not only would he be reckless, and daily given to making blots in the afternoon, but, some days, he went further, and was rather noisy." Nippers, the second clerk, was "a whiskered, sallow, and, upon the whole, rather piratical-looking young man." He spent much of the day adjusting the height and angle of his

desk. His employer also complained of Nippers' "diseased ambition," which was "evinced by a certain impatience of the duties of a mere copyist, and unwarrantable usurpation of strictly
professional affairs, such as the drawing up of legal documents." No doubt Nippers put these documents to his own
use, for he was "considerable of a ward politician, [and] occasionally did a little business at the Justices' courts. . . . Ginger
Nut, the third on my list, was a lad, some twelve years old. His
father was a car-man, ambitious of seeing his son on the bench
instead of a cart, before he died. So he sent him to my office, as
student at law, errand-boy, cleaner and sweeper, at the rate of
one dollar a week. He had a little desk to himself, but he did
not use it much. . . . Not the least among the employments of
Ginger Nut, as well as one which he discharged with the most
alacrity, was his duty as cake and apple purveyor for Turkey
and Nippers."[1]

The main clerical work done in this lawyer's office, where
documents often had to be reproduced in triplicate or more,
was copying. The work in other offices of that day may have
been more heavily concentrated on other tasks, such as bookkeeping, depending on the firm in question. But their small
scale was a characteristic common to all pre–Civil War offices,
reflecting the political economy of the time.

Prior to the Civil War, the United States was overwhelmingly
agrarian.[2] Most rural Americans produced for their own use—
they planted and harvested their own grain, vegetables, and
fruits; raised, slaughtered, and cured their own meat; ate the
eggs of their own chickens; drank the milk of their own cows.
Any surplus was sold to buy goods not produced in the household, such as horseshoes, wagons, or metal cooking ware.
These were bought in the nearest town, or on occasion from a
traveling peddler, and, by and large, were produced locally.
There were very few enterprises geared to the national market,
and those that were were hampered by a distributive network
that was rudimentary and slow. Until the 1820s, when the first
canals were dug, goods traveled over roads or natural water-

ways. It was not until the 1850s that railroad lines started to stretch over more than a few miles; the golden spike that marked the connection of the east and west coasts was not hammered in until 1869.

Nonetheless, some enterprises operated on a national scale. Insurance companies, for example, got their start as supportive institutions for the commerce and shipping that flourished in east coast seaports around 1800. Merchants and shipowners did a brisk trade in the transport and sale of southern cotton and tobacco, manufactured goods from Britain, tea and spices from China, rum and sugar from the West Indies, and, last but by no means least, African slaves. In order to protect themselves from the financial disasters of shipwreck and piracy, these merchants insured their boats and cargo.[3] Banks also operated on a regional or national scale. They often had branches in several cities and issued their own currency, which resulted in some chaos since the actual worth of any particular banknote varied widely. After 1836, when the Second National Bank lost its charter, there were no national banks, and the era of "wildcat banking" began, lasting until 1863. The currencies of state and municipal banks, however, still circulated throughout the country.[4]

Some industrial firms also produced for regional markets before the Civil War. Located primarily in New England, these factories produced mainly cotton and woolen cloth. Samuel Slater established the first spinning mill in 1790, in Pawtucket, Rhode Island; over twenty years later the first mill combining all the textile manufacturing processes—carding, spinning, and weaving—was built in Waltham, Massachusetts. A group of Boston sea merchants, whose trade had been severely handicapped by the European wars and the War of 1812, were looking for new ways of investing their capital. Their venture was considered a daring one at the time. English textile factories had a fifty-year headstart and dominated the cloth market. But the Boston Manufacturing Company built their mill nonetheless and very quickly made a success of it. They did not, however, try to compete with the English manufacturers in the production of finely woven or beautifully dyed cloth. Instead they concentrated on rough sheeting, much of which was turned into clothing for slaves in the South.[5]

Industrial manufacturing, then, had taken firm root in New England by the Civil War, but it did not yet dominate the American political economy. Antebellum enterprises were still quite small and limited to a local market. Small-town merchants mainly sold their wares to local folk. In large towns and cities, numerous dry goods merchants with modest operations competed for customers—large department stores were not established until the latter part of the nineteenth century. This pattern for the merchandising of dry goods was duplicated in any number of commercial concerns.

The prevalence of small businesses in turn held down the size of office staffs. Even the larger enterprises mentioned above—insurance companies, banks, and some factories— hired only a few clerks. Despite the small size of pre–Civil War offices, however, it is possible to differentiate among the various kinds of office work.

Office Jobs

A copyist, or scrivener as he was sometimes called, did exactly what his name implies—he copied. Working from the rough draft of a letter or legal document, he would copy it out in a fine hand, using a quill pen and drying the freshly written ink with sand. He would also often proofread the documents he copied, as Melville notes in "Bartleby." "Where there are two or more scriveners in an office, they assist each other in this examination, one reading from the copy, the other holding the original."[6] A copyist's primary skill, therefore, was penmanship, the ability to write a neat and legible hand. The more quickly he could write, of course, the better. If he was an accurate speller who could catch mistakes in his employer's rough draft, well and good, although this does not seem to have been an absolute requirement of the job.

A lawyer's business generally warranted hiring at least one copyist. The attorney who handled a real estate transaction, for example, would probably have at least four copies of the official transaction drawn up—one each for the seller, the buyer, the public records office, and himself. It is easy to imagine the amount of copying that even a moderately prosperous lawyer would require.

Other enterprises, however, did not involve as much paper-work and might employ a clerk who counted copying only as one among several skills and duties. Thomas Hancock was a prominent eighteenth-century Boston merchant whose ships sailed to England as well as the West Indies and who had many business contacts in both places. Some of the cargo brought back to Boston by his vessels was sold in his store. Hancock had a "compting room" where the routine office work was handled by clerks, although his nephew John once complained that he was "reduced at the last Moment to write my own letters." In general, the Hancocks would write the rough draft of a letter on any available scrap of paper; their clerks were then to make the final copy. Foreign letters were also copied into the letter book. The Hancocks insured against loss at sea by having additional copies of foreign correspondence sent by later boats.[7]

In the offices of merchants, it would seem, copying was not the meticulous or painstaking affair that it was likely to be where a copyist was employed as such for the express purpose of transcribing documents. "Frequently [the letters from Hancock's office] were dashed off at the last moment before a ship sailed, and bear traces of scurry; many contain phrases such as 'Inclosed we send you an original Letter from Mr. Winslow as we have no Time to copy it,' and 'the sudden Departure of this Vessell prevents my writing to ——.'"[8] The Baltimore merchant Robert Oliver, whose fortune amounted to over a million dollars at the time of his death, was one of the richest men in the country. "He generally composed the letters, except possibly routine ones, that their clerk William Knight copied into the Letter Books at the countinghouse on Second Street. Robert did some of the copying himself. . . ."[9]

The copyist hired only to copy letters and documents was analogous to the typist in the post–Civil War office. Although the job ideally required the ability to write in a clear hand, it was not one that carried much responsibility. Nor did it afford opportunities for gaining experience and competence in a wide variety of office tasks, in contrast to such office jobs as the general clerk or bookkeeper. The author of the *House of Hancock* suggests that copying was not considered to be a complicated job. When John Hancock was first brought into his uncle's firm during the French and Indian Wars, "he is hardly mentioned in the business papers, and there is no sign of his having done anything more responsible than make neat copies in his uncle's letter book."[10] While a copyist restricted to this chore would undoubtedly learn about the firm's business practices from its letters and documents, he would not gain much practical experience in other aspects of office work, such as keeping the books, extracting money from debtors, evading creditors, or even composing letters. However, many firms did not seem to have enough paperwork to merit hiring someone for the exclusive purpose of copying, and much of it was done by clerks as one among many office tasks.

Copying was not viewed as complicated work requiring a good deal of training, but such was not the case with bookkeeping. The bookkeeper kept the financial records of his firm. These records, at the minimum, were a written accounting of financial transactions and of debts and credits. At the maximum, a firm's ledgers provide an easy-to-read picture of assets and liabilities, the state of financial relations with any other businesses, and the profit or loss incurred by any particular venture. The practice of keeping written accounts goes back to antiquity, but principles of double-entry bookkeeping, which lie at the root of modern bookkeeping, were first written down by a Venetian monk, Luca Paciolo, in 1494.[11]

Although a codified system of double-entry bookkeeping existed, it was not always used. It was not unusual for Thomas Hancock, in the firm's early days, to accept payment in kind (such as grain, livestock, or other produce), which he either consumed himself or sold in his store. If he deemed that the payment squared the debt in question, he was unlikely to enter the transaction in his ledger. Neither Thomas nor his nephew John Hancock was in the habit of recording more than outstanding debts or credits in his ledgers. Thus many of the Hancocks' financial transactions were simply never written down, and their books hardly reflected a complete picture of their dealings.[12] According to Matthew Josephson, some highly successful nineteenth-century capitalists dispensed with a bookkeeper altogether. Cornelius Vanderbilt "had no recognizable system for running his railroads; his books were kept in his head, or in an old cigar box, according to some reports; yet so parsimonious, so stern in management was he that he was never to lose a day's interest on the smallest of sums."[13] And about Daniel Drew: "This 'Sphinx of the Stock Market' was as suspicious as Vanderbilt, also kept all his accounts in his head and considered the whole paraphernalia of bookkeeping a confounded fraud."[14]

This absence of a single method of bookkeeping does not mean that each firm developed its own system from scratch. For example, bookkeeping courses were taught in some high schools before the Civil War. John D. Rockefeller studied bookkeeping at Cleveland's Central High School in the 1850s, and, at sixteen, worked as a bookkeeper for a produce merchant on the city's docks. Bookkeepers were also trained through various forms of apprenticeship. In 1835 the young Jay Cooke went to work as a clerk in a dry goods, grocery, and hardware store in Sandusky, Ohio. "His salary was $250 a year. He stayed with this firm one year, during which time, in the lei-

sure of winter days when there was little trade, he learned
double-entry bookkeeping from one of the partners, and also
chess."[15] In Dreiser's *The Financier*, Frank Cowperwood, a
ruthless Philadelphia capitalist, started out as an apprentice
bookkeeper.[16]

Whether a bookkeeper learned the trade in school or on
the job as an apprentice, he was in a commanding position to
understand the practices of his firm. Unlike the twentieth-
century clerical worker, a bookkeeper in a pre–Civil War business was acquainted with all of its financial dealings and records, rather than being restricted to a single specialized department that paid bills, or sent bills, or credited accounts, and
so on. Antebellum firms were simply not large enough to necessitate breaking their office operations down into different
sections. Thus a bookkeeper understood the entire scope of a
business's operations and his books disclosed a complete picture of its finances (to the extent, of course, that complete
books were kept.)

The messenger, errand boy, or office boy, as he was vari-
ously named, was another fixture of the antebellum office
staff. Ginger Nut, of Melville's "Bartleby," was just such an
office boy, although his main duty seems to have been going
out to buy cookies for the copyists. Most office boys were
charged with a variety of other tasks as well. Since there were
no telephones, an office boy would be dispatched to carry a
message to another firm or person, and often would wait to
bring back a reply. He also served as a delivery boy, carrying
copies of documents to the various interested parties. He procured supplies for the office, including everything from food to
quill pens; and had housekeeping duties as well, such as refill-
ing ink wells, keeping pots filled with fresh sand for the copyists to dry their manuscripts, and sweeping up and dusting at
the beginning or end of the work day. In short, the office boy
did not have a prescribed set of routine tasks. Rather, his main
responsibility was to be available for any minor task that might
arise. Although he would usually spend his day doing rela-

tively menial work—running personal errands and keeping the office clean—he was not chained to his desk in the monotonous execution of the same assignment. Most office boys were just that, boys, and their job was only a steppingstone to a clerkship.

Clerks were by far the largest occupational group in antebellum offices. Their duties were quite varied, their tasks depending upon the kind of firm that employed them. Jay Cooke, in his early years as a clerk for the Washington Packet and Transportation Company in Philadelphia, "kept books, solicited trade, handled publicity for the company, and served as general assistant."[17] A year later, as a broker's clerk, he wrote with a clear hand, figured with accuracy and speed, and did bookkeeping.[18]

Thus, clerks had a wide range of tasks. At the end of the War of 1812, a Massachusetts shipowner and merchant, anxious to get his ships under way, gave the following directions to his clerks: "Go out and collect as many laborers as possible to go up river; Charles, do you go and find Mr. _____, the rigger, and Mr. _____, the sail-maker, and tell them I want to see them immediately; John, go and engage half a dozen truckmen for today and to-morrow; Stephen, hunt up as many caulkers and gravers as you can find, and engage them to work."[19] One of "A Great Merchant's Recollections of Old New York" was of his early-morning duties as a merchant's clerk: "It was a very different thing, in those days, to be a boy in a store from what it is now . . . I had to go every morning to Vanderwater Street for the keys, as my employers must have them in case of fire in the night. There was much ambition among the young men as to who should have his store opened first, and I used to be up soon after light, walk to Vanderwater Street and then to the store very early. It was to be sprinkled with water, which I brought the evening before from the old pump at the corner of Peck Slip and Pearl Street, then carefully swept and dusted. Then came sprinkling the sidewalk and street, and sweeping to the center a heap for the dirtcart to remove.

This done, one of the older clerks would come, and I would be permitted to go home for breakfast. In winter the wood was to be carried and piled in the cellar, fires were to be made, and lamps trimmed. I mention these particulars to show that junior clerks in those days did the work now done by the porters." [20]

The typical clerk was thus afforded an opportunity to demonstrate his competence in many aspects of office work. Such was Jay Cooke's experience in the Philadelphia brokerage firm. "Though the firm was small and its equipment simple, it had one great advantage for Jay: it gave him an opportunity to show what he could do. In such a concern as the Clark house, it was to be expected that the young clerk would have varied duties and would be given responsibilities if found equal to them. Among other things, he at first served as messenger and delivery boy, going to banks on business for the Clarks." He soon served as teller and, after a year, wrote letters, sometimes fifteen or twenty a day. Within two years, Cooke had so proved himself that the partners granted him power of attorney to sign for the firm. [21]

With the exception of those who were employed purely as copyists, pre–Civil War office workers engaged in a wide variety of tasks. Their duties ranged from drafting letters to keeping the books to carrying messages from one part of town to another. Even a bookkeeper whose primary responsibility was maintaining a firm's financial records concerned himself with all aspects of those records, instead of being confined to one small bailiwick in a bookkeeping department. Insofar as pre–Civil War office workers were in a position to master the entire scope of an office's operations, they were not unlike craftsmen engaged in the various manual crafts. Ideally a craftsman understood and was proficient at all aspects of the work that went into the particular product. If one considers a well-run office or a well-kept set of books to be the "product," it is possible to see many pre–Civil War clerks as craftsmen, proficient at all aspects of running an office or of bookkeeping. The work was organized as an integrated whole, rather than being broken down into a series of component parts separate from one another. This important characteristic of antebellum office work was one that it shared with the private secretary's job in the expanded office of the late nineteenth and twentieth centuries. The private secretary was also given responsibility for a wide range of duties and was in a position to gain a good deal of understanding about his or her employer and firm. But there is one major difference between the pre–Civil War clerk and the twentieth-century private secretary: the knowledge gained by the clerk in the course of his extensive duties could aid him in advancing in the business world. The twentieth-century private secretary, by contrast, was to find his, and particularly her, chances for advancement severely curtailed.

Relations between Clerks and Employers

Since most antebellum offices were very small, the chain of command was very simple. Usually the employer told his two or three clerks what to do; orders were not passed down a complex hierarchical ladder or funneled through successive departments.[22] The tenor of office relations, however, was influenced by the personalities of both employer and, to a lesser extent, employees. The lawyer in "Bartleby" seems to have been a rather kindly but ineffectual boss: he was unable to control his irascible clerks and tried to accommodate their idiosyncratic quirks rather than give them the boot. Dickens's Scrooge, on the other hand, was the prototypical taskmaster, keeping his clerk at his desk to the last possible second, even on Christmas Eve, and irritated that custom forced him to give the clerk a vacation day on Christmas itself.[23] A clerk in 1841 wrote: "So much of a man's character in after life depends on what kind of an employer he had when he was young, that it is worthy of being much more seriously considered by parents and young men than it is. How often do we see men, in whom we can trace the effect of this kind of education, and see the exact resemblance of their former masters in the manners, thoughts, habits, and vices, which they have copied unaware! Happily we sometimes see virtues, too, and can trace their foundation to the same sources."[24]

The personal nature of the employer's control of his clerks was reinforced by the lack of common standards of office procedure: each employer developed his own. Furthermore, his directives were not mediated by machines, nor did machines set the pace of work. The office was unlike the factory workplace, where workers might conclude that the machine rather than its owner ran them at a certain pace, and where, consequently, blame for arduous working conditions might be shifted from the employer, thereby obscuring class relations. Since there were no office machines in the antebellum office, there was no opportunity for the personal directives of the employers to be transformed into the impersonal directives of a machine.

Another important element of office relations was trust between employer and office worker. There are numerous references to "trusted employees" in writings about the pre–Civil War office. In *The Financier*, Dreiser sets up a running comparison between Frank Cowperwood, the unscrupulous and therefore rapidly successful financier, and his father, Henry, whose honesty is unimpeachable but whose fortune is not nearly so great as his son's. After many years of faithful work as a clerk in a bank, Henry Cowperwood is promoted to teller, and it is suggested that his trustworthiness earns him this promotion. Then there are the liabilities attached to *not* being trustworthy. Jay Gould, a late nineteenth-century railroad magnate, worked in his youth as clerk to a village storekeeper. Learning that his employer was planning to buy a certain property for $2,000, Gould borrowed money from his father, got in ahead of his employer, and bought the tract for $2,500. Two weeks later he sold it again for $4,000. "But his employer, it appears, was highly incensed at what he saw as trickery or duplicity in his assistant and summarily dismissed him."[25]

And a final example: writing in 1842, a clerk exhorted merchants to have trust in his kind:

> The interest which clerks generally feel in the business and success of their employers, is, I believe, estimated too cheaply; and that many feel so little, is, perhaps, as often the fault of their employers as their own. The majority of clerks are young men who have hopes and prospects of business before them. They have not yet thrown off that trusting confidence and generous friendship peculiar to youth—they are disposed to think well of themselves and the world, and they feel it deeply when too great a distance is maintained between themselves and their superiors. . . .
>
> A good clerk feels that he has an interest in the credit and success of his employer beyond the amount of his salary; and with the close of every successful year, he feels that he too, by his assiduity and fidelity, has added something to his capital—something to his future prospects, and something to his support if overtaken with adversity; and a good merchant encourages and reciprocates all these feelings.[26]

To a certain extent, personal trust was necessitated by the very nature of the office. The bulk of office work, as noted above, was written work—copying out letters and documents, adding up columns of figures, computing and sending out bills, keeping accurate records of financial transactions. If an employer wanted to check up on each employee's work to make sure it was being done correctly, he had to spend most of his day overseeing the staff. The only way to be sure that a bookkeeper or clerk had tallied a column of numbers accurately was for the employer to repeat the task himself. But there was a way of avoiding a large investment of time in surveillance: an employer might establish a relationship with his clerks such that he could *trust* them to do their work correctly without much supervision.

Another source of trust between employer and clerk lay in the apprenticeship system, which was prevalent throughout the eighteenth century, and may well have extended into the nineteenth. The author of *Daniel Henchman, A Colonial Book-*

seller indicates that many clerical duties were performed by youths taken on as apprentices for a particular business. "Daniel Henchman was born in Boston in 1689. Nothing is known about his early life, but on the assumption that he served the normal seven-year apprenticeship, we may conclude that he would set up as an independent bookseller about 1710."[27] The same author notes elsewhere that "it was usual for a merchant to send his son to work in the countinghouse of a distant correspondent, in order that the boy might be trained in business."[28] The eighteenth-century Hancocks would often take in the children of their agents in foreign ports, either simply for boarding or for learning the business. "Again, a Jamaica correspondent asks Thomas to board one child, who is still at school, and to take another into the countinghouse ('let me know what you would Ask with him & I'll remit you sugar or Molasses for that purpose, before I send him over')."[29] Evidence that some clerks were still considered apprentices in the nineteenth century comes from "Familiar Scenes in the Life of a Clerk," where mention is made of a "gentleman [who] lived in an eastern seaport town, and was a grocer, doing a considerable business. He had a boy apprenticed to him, whose name was John"—and who is thereafter referred to as the "grocer's clerk."[30]

An employer who took on an apprentice was not, ideally at least, simply hiring labor. (In fact, as the Jamaica correspondent indicated, apprentices often paid their employer for the training they were to receive.) He was also taking on the responsibility of giving a young boy good training in a trade, and of providing what was often paternal guidance. Understandably, then, the personalities of both employer and apprentice would figure prominently in their relations, and there might well exist a good deal of trust between them. Thus, to the extent that clerks in pre–Civil War offices were considered apprentices, it is not surprising that the relations between them and their employers were heavily affected by individual personalities and by the expectation of mutual trust. Clerk apprentices also shared another feature of apprenticeships: they were promoted to management or ownership positions at the end of their indenture. Even when formal apprenticeships were no longer being granted, the attitudes and standards of behavior that had accompanied them were not likely to fade away immediately.

The significance of the personal nature of the relations between employer and clerk, where trust was such an important element, is that the class differences between the two were likely to be obscured. In the first place, the typical clerk would perceive his situation in personal, rather than class, terms. If he worked for a particularly hard taskmaster, he might harbor feelings of rebelliousness. But his analysis of the situation would probably focus on personality—his employer's greed, meanness, cruelty, and so on—rather than on the larger structure, wherein clerks sold their labor power to employers who profited from it. Since the emphasis was on the employer's personal shortcomings, the clerk would be more likely to search for a kindlier employer than to attempt to band together with fellow clerks in protest against harsh conditions. An English commentator, writing at the end of the nineteenth century, accepts this personalization as *prima facie* evidence that clerks would not unionize: "For clerks a trade union has no attraction. Its advantages are not apparent, the relationship between employer and employed being in this case essentially personal."[31]

The emphasis on trust between employer and employee only served to strengthen the tendency to personalize their relationship. An employer who stressed trust for his employee was establishing their relationship on a friendly, even if not equal, footing. The employee, in turn, may well have responded to such an arrangement by trying either to earn or to keep this trust. If trust, and perhaps even friendship, emerged as dominant features, it was unlikely that the relationship would be seen as antagonistic.

This tradition of personalism and trust persisted and continued to affect the relations between employer and clerk long after the antebellum office had been supplanted by later forms. But it was not only the centrality of personal relations that blurred class differences. Another, and possibly more important, factor was the opportunity for upward mobility that was available to at least some pre–Civil War clerks.

Upward Mobility among Clerks

After learning the business of the firm to which they were attached, apprenticed clerks often became owners or managers themselves. This was particularly true in the eighteenth century. John Hancock was a case in point. Brought into his uncle's firm in the 1750s, young Hancock was at first given only minor office work. "But . . . Thomas decided that his nephew must have a bigger hand in management. The most urgent task of the moment was to make the government honor its bills. So in 1760 John was put aboard a ship bound for London, with the triple idea that he might act as debt-collector-extraordinary, make friends with English agents, and see something of Europe as befitted a young gentleman." [32] Upon his return to Boston, John Hancock was made a partner in his uncle's firm. The apprenticed grocer's clerk mentioned above "became devoted to his master's business as if it had been his own, gained his entire confidence, and, although but an apprentice boy, without money and friends, in return for his devotion, the day he was twenty-one years old, he was made a partner in an extensive concern, with a large capital." [33]

To be sure, many clerk apprentices who later rose to positions of management or ownership came from families that already were of the merchant or other propertied class. John Hancock, for one, was a nephew of the merchant who took him on. [34] But there is evidence indicating that upward mobility, in the United States at least, was not reserved solely for such clerks. John Hancock's "1766 expansion program included the starting of a shop, to serve as a retail counterpart for the main business. He appointed one of his clerks called Palfrey as its manager, on a profit-sharing basis; he imported some £1,800 worth of stock-in-trade for this protégé, and also gave him an extra-warm recommendation to Barnard and Harrison so that further goods might be ordered from London direct."[35] One of "A Great Merchant's Recollections of Old New York" is of how he got his start in his own firm. As a clerk he had done business with a merchant from Connecticut, who proposed that the author go into partnership with his son, a recent Yale graduate whom his father "was anxious to place in New York." The new venture's initial capital was provided in the main by the Connecticut merchant, while the author contributed the small amount he had saved, mostly from his salary. Thus did one clerk begin his move up in the business world.[36] Finally, Jay Cooke's biographer remarks upon Jay's being made a partner in a Philadelphia brokerage house at the age of twenty-one: "In view of the fact that young Cooke made no contribution of capital, his membership in the firm was clearly in recognition of his ability."[37]

It would be wrong to leave the impression that upward mobility via a clerkship was available to all. The men who could obtain jobs as clerks in the first place came largely from situations of some advantage. Stephan Thernstrom has observed of nineteenth-century Newburyport that clerks were of necessity educated men. Hence their families must have been sufficiently well off to forego their sons' potential earnings and send them to school instead.[38] Furthermore, clerks were predominantly native-born at a time when immigrants were swelling the population. In mid-nineteenth-century Boston, Oscar Handlin has found, 88.2 percent of the city's clerks were native-born, while only 3.6 percent were Irish immigrants.[39]

While upward mobility undoubtedly existed for antebellum office clerks, it is difficult to be precise about how widespread those opportunities were. Possibly the chance to move up was greater when the clerk-apprentice system was prevalent and diminished somewhat as the system declined.

The implications of upward mobility for clerks were clear. First, that many clerks were really apprentice owners or managers meant that their class position was complex. They were the antebellum analogues of today's business school student or management trainee. Then, too, there were those who never attained positions of ownership but were trusted and competent office managers. Their grasp of office details, and their ability to take the initiative and make decisions on their own, enabled them to become masters in the craft of office management. Harry Braverman writes that "the clerical employees of the early nineteenth-century enterprise may, on the whole, more properly appear as the ancestors of modern professional management than of the present classification of clerical workers."[40] And yet there were surely some clerks, particularly copyists, who had neither a grasp of the basics of office management nor much chance of upward mobility. But it would have been difficult to differentiate on other than a purely personal basis between their class situations: an enterprising copyist might well be moved into the more responsible position of clerk-cum-office manager; and even clerks of humble background had opportunities to own businesses or go into partnership.

This ambiguous class position of clerks could have a profound effect on their class identity. If they believed that it was possible to move upward, they were likely to focus on how to get ahead rather than on the common problems shared by all clerks. Writing about England, David Lockwood analyzes the effect of promoting able clerical workers of working-class origins: "The example of these successful clerks must have always been a spur to the individualistic strivings of the younger clerks, while for the older and unsuccessful ones yet another confirmation that their own lowly positions were due entirely to their own deficiencies."[41] There were strong pressures on a clerk encouraging him to think of himself as an individual with a real chance of upward mobility, and not as a permanent member of his class.

The fact that many managers and owners had started out as clerks created an ideology about clerks that survived long after the facts no longer warranted it. As late as the turn of the century, the conventional wisdom had it that the way to succeed in business was to start out as a clerk. By this time the examples of clerks being promoted to positions of ownership or high-level management had become very rare indeed. But the ideology born in the pre–Civil War years died hard.

It is not through oversight that I have used masculine pronouns in referring to pre–Civil War clerks. For they were all men. The office of this era was a male preserve. This would not last, however. During the Civil War the first records of women being employed as office workers appeared.

3

Office Work
after the Civil War

The last third of the nineteenth century witnessed drastic changes in the scale and shape of business enterprise. The small and highly competitive firms that had dominated production in the antebellum United States gave way to giant corporations integrated vertically and horizontally in the merger movement that swept through industry during the 1890s. In the steel, oil, tobacco, food, and meat-packing sectors, to name just a few, such corporations enjoyed virtual monopolies.

As is now well known, profound changes in production techniques accompanied the rise of the trusts. But innovation was not restricted to the shop floor. It also reached upwards into the office, for the increase in the volume of business, coupled with the development of regional, national, and international markets, led to a proliferation of correspondence and inspired the need for more accurate record keeping. As the amount and geographic range of a firm's activities grew, it became more difficult for that firm to conduct the bulk of its transactions in person. While face-to-face business contacts by no means disappeared, a businessman might choose to pay a bill, order merchandise, or confirm an appointment in writing rather than in person, particularly when the transaction took place between cities. Even after the invention of the telephone, many businesses preferred to keep a written record of transactions rather than having to rely on memory.

As a firm's operations expanded and became more complex, accurate records of its transactions became more important. A small entrepreneurial butcher did not need very complex records. He might keep a list of which customers owed him money and how much, and of how many pounds of beef and how many pounds of pork he could expect each week from various meat-slaughterers, but he would not need much more. A large meat-packing firm, however, required more complex records: how many head of cattle were fattening in pens in Omaha or Kansas City, and how many were being driven across the plains from points farther west; how much the workers in the slaughterhouses were being paid; how many refrigerated cars were on their way to the eastern cities, and how many on their way back. These records had to be accurate and up-to-date, for the managers needed detailed information at their fingertips in order to make plans for the future. Furthermore, as Harry Braverman has pointed out, firms required elaborate records to guard against fraud both by their own employees and by the companies with which they did business.[1]

Among the outstanding features of the reorganization of the office was the division of businesses into departments.[2] This became necessary as firms grew so large and complex that it was no longer possible for one capitalist, or even a small group, to make all the decisions. The ultimate control of a firm's capital and direction still rested with the owner or owners, but the more mundane operations were decentralized into various functionally defined departments. The Pennsylvania Railroad management, for example, one of the first to introduce this method of organization, instituted separate offices for accounting and for the supervision of roadbeds and moving stock. It also worked out a more elaborate structure of relations between the major departments and their ancillary units.[3]

These organizational innovations were accompanied by the

subdivision of clerical labor. Before the Civil War there had been four basic clerical jobs in the office: copyist, bookkeeper, messenger or office boy, and clerk. This relatively simple range of occupations was expanded and elaborated following the war, with the division of labor most pronounced in the largest offices. File clerks, shipping clerks, billing clerks and other "semiskilled" workers began to appear. The exact pattern that the division of labor followed in a particular office depended, of course, on the nature of the business at hand. An insurance company might have many billing or file clerks, but no shipping clerks whatsoever; a mail-order house would use an army of shipping and file clerks, but no billing clerks since orders were paid in advance.

Not surprisingly, the most popular change resulted from the introduction of the typewriter. Once it was adopted, stenographers and typists quite rapidly replaced copyists. A stenographer's job consisted of taking dictation, usually from a firm's manager or owner, although occasionally also from a higher-level clerical worker, and then transcribing the notes into a letter, report, or whatever. For a while, it was considered rude or disrespectful for a firm to type its correspondence, and some dictation was at first transcribed in a fine longhand. Before long, however, typewriting became the accepted mode of business correspondence, and handwritten letters yielded to typewritten ones. The stenographer was in effect a direct replacement for a copyist, since in general stenography encompassed transcription as well as dictation. The integration of these tasks came about not only because many different systems of shorthand were in use, but also because stenographers tended to add individual quirks or shortcuts to the system being used. Hence the stenographer might be the only one who could read his or her notes. At first glance it would seem that the shift from copyist to stenographer involved no further division of labor. But the fact that typists were being hired as well as stenographers suggests even greater specialization. Take the example of a manufacturer with outstanding debts from thirty customers. He might decide to send each of them a dunning letter couched in the strongest language instead of an invoice with "Third and Final Notice" stamped on it in red ink. He might dictate this letter to a stenographer, who would transcribe it in longhand and pass it on, along with the names and addresses of the overdue debtors, to two or three typists, who would produce as many copies of the letter as necessary. The result was that what had once been done by one kind of clerk, a copyist, was now done by two, a stenographer and a typist. In this example, the typists execute the bulk of the task at hand, and the manufacturer congratulates himself on the efficiency of his system and on the money saved by using a stenographer only where necessary and by using typists whenever possible.

This increasing division of labor constituted a basic change in the organization of office work. In antebellum offices clerical workers were responsible for a wide range of tasks and in some cases their work bore the aspects of a craft. But the division and redivision of clerical tasks meant that an individual clerical worker performed only a small number of tasks in a larger range of operations. This reorganization of work was uneven. It first appeared immediately before the Civil War (the Erie Railroad) and was clearly taking hold by the 1870s.[4] Thus the post-Civil War expansion and consolidation of capitalism drastically rearranged the office by partitioning firms into departments and dividing up clerical work into specialized tasks. Another factor which did much to alter the appearance of clerical work, and which had some influence on the changing nature of that work, was technological innovation, with the typewriter being far and away the most important of the new office machines.[5]

The Typewriter

The first record of an attempt to make a writing machine dates to 1714, when the Englishman Henry Mill obtained a patent

for "an artificial machine or method for the impressing or transcribing of letters singly or progressively one after another, as
in writing, whereby all writings whatsoever may be engrossed
in paper or parchment so neat and exact as not to be distinguished from print."[6] Over the next one hundred and fifty
years, numerous inventors followed in Mill's footsteps. The
first American to do so was William Austin Burt of Michigan.
Curiously enough, the basic principle of his machine was essentially the same as that found in "selectrics," the newest of
contemporary typewriters: "the type was mounted on a rotat-
ing, semicircular frame, not on individual type bars, and the
idea was to move the wheel around until the desired letter
came to the printing point. Then it was pressed down against
the paper with a lever."[7] Burt showed his machine to a friend,
John P. Sheldon, editor of a Detroit newspaper, who was so
taken with the invention and its possibilities that he wrote to
President Andrew Jackson in 1829:

> Sir:
> This is a specimen of the printing done by me on Mr. Burt's
> typographer. You will observe some inaccuracies in the situation
> of the letters; these are owing to the imperfections of the ma-
> chine, it having been made in the woods of Michigan where no
> proper tools could be obtained by the inventor. . . . I am satisfied,
> from my knowledge of the printing business, as well as from the
> operation of the rough machine, with which I am now printing,
> that the typographer will be ranked with the most novel, useful
> and pleasing inventions of this age.[8]

Burt's machine had one major drawback: it was slower than
writing by hand. This, perhaps, was the reason that Burt and
Sheldon could find no one in Detroit or New York to finance
the perfection and manufacture of the typographer. A more
fundamental reason for their failure, however, is that in the
1830s the potential value of a writing machine was not readily
apparent to businessmen who ran small offices with a few
clerks and a relatively small amount of paperwork. Only after

the Civil War did an inventor of a writing machine succeed in finding financial backing for it.

That inventor was Christopher Latham Sholes of Milwaukee, Wisconsin. Although Sholes is generally referred to as the "Father of the Typewriter," this is inaccurate, since he was preceded by many others who invented writing machines of various types. According to Bruce Bliven, who relies on the files of claims for patent rights, Sholes was actually the fifty-second man to invent the typewriter.[9] A printer, publisher, and civil servant from Milwaukee, Sholes was also an amateur inventor. He first tried his hand at a writing machine in 1867 after reading about another version in *Scientific American*. By 1869 Sholes was convinced that he and two co-workers had ironed all the kinks out of their machine, and he typed this letter to James Densmore, an acquaintance who was interested in promoting inventions.

> You will recollect that in all of our discussions touching a machine for writing, we have held to several fundamental ideas, as essential to success. For instance, that the machine must be simple and not liable to get out of order; that it must work easily and be susceptible of being worked rapidly; and finally, that it be made with reasonable cheapness. To supersede an instrument as handy as the pen every one of these conditions is essential and a failure in any is fatal. The failure of all previous efforts in this direction—which I find on research have been many—are all to be ascribed to a lack in some one of these particulars.[10]

Sholes believed that his machine had satisfied all his conditions, but Densmore, who by this point had started to provide ready cash for the Sholes group and had entered into a formal partnership with them, was skeptical. For the next few years, their dealings amounted to Densmore insisting on yet further improvements, Sholes grudgingly making them, and Densmore still not being satisfied.

Finally, even Densmore was convinced that the machine was workable. The remaining stumbling block was raising enough capital to finance mass production of the Sholes proto-type. Densmore and Sholes had made several attempts to in-terest a promoter, and while there had been several nibbles, there were no takers. At last Densmore appealed in desperation to his brother Amos for funds, arguing that "the atmosphere is full of aspirations for making a typewriter," and stressing that, if they did not act quickly, they would be beaten out by others, including the likes of Thomas Alva Edison.[11]

With the money he raised from his brother, Densmore set up shop in Milwaukee, and production was under way by the summer of 1872. The next step was to distribute the machines as widely as possible, in order that the typewriter might be-come more familiar in offices, thereby increasing demand. He did manage to sell all of the machines produced in 1872, most of them to telegraphers and shorthand reporters. Government employees and businessmen bought almost none.

Although he sold all of his machines, Densmore made no profits. Still in search of financial backing, he approached the firm of E. Remington and Sons, who were gunmakers in Ilion, New York. The Remington factory was relatively sophisti-cated, and many of its operations could be adapted to making Densmore's machine. The Remington executives were inter-ested in the typewriter but drove a hard bargain.

> Remington asked Benedict, according to the latter's recollection:
> "What do you think of it?"
> "That machine is very crude," Benedict replied, "but there is an idea there that will revolutionize business."
> "Do you think we ought to take it up?"
> "We must on no account let it get away. It isn't necessary to tell these people that we are crazy over the invention, but I'm afraid I am pretty nearly so."[12]

After some negotiating, Remington agreed to manufacture one thousand machines, Densmore paid an advance of ten thousand dollars, and they signed a contract on 1 March 1873. In the spring of 1874, the first machines were finished, and

Densmore set out to promote them to Manhattan businessmen for $125 apiece. Sales agencies were set up across the
United States but only 400 had been sold by the end of 1874.
By and large, purchasers were those who were intrigued by
the idea and who could afford to spend $125. Typewriters did
not spread like wildfire through the nation's business offices.
One of the first customers was Mark Twain, who saw a typewriter in a Boston shopwindow and went in to inquire. The
salesman set his "type girl" to work demonstrating the machine. Impressed by the fact that the demonstrator typed fifty-
seven words a minute, Twain bought it on the spot. Upon
returning to his hotel, accompanied by his friend and fellow
humorist Petroleum V. Nasby, Twain soon felt that he had been
gypped, and as he recounted in his autobiography:

> We got our slips [upon which the demonstrator had typed her
> fifty-seven words per minute] and were a little disappointed to
> find that they all contained the same words. The girl had econo-
> mized time and labor by memorizing a formula which she knew
> by heart.
>
> At home I played with the toy, repeating and repeating and re-
> peating "The boy stood on the burning deck" until I could turn out
> that boy's adventure at the rate of twelve words a minute; then I
> resumed the pen for business, and only worked the machine to as-
> tonish inquisitive visitors. They carried off reams of the boy and
> his burning deck.[13]

This was how Twain remembered the affair many years after-
ward. At the time he waxed considerably more enthusiastic, as
in this letter to his brother (which indicates that Twain's typewriter had only upper-case letters, as was true of the early
machines):

DEAR BROTHER:
I AM TRYING TO GET THE HANG OF THIS NEW FANGLED
WRITING MACHINE, BUT I AM NOT MAKING A SHINING
SUCCESS OF IT. HOWEVER THIS IS THE FIRST ATTEMPT
I HAVE EVER MADE & YET I PERCEIVE I SHALL SOON &
EASILY ACQUIRE A FINE FACILITY IN ITS USE. . . . THE

MACHINE HAS SEVERAL VIRTUES. I BELIEVE IT WILL
PRINT FASTER THAN I CAN WRITE. ONE MAY LEAN BACK
ON HIS CHAIR & AND WORK IT. IT PILES AN AWFUL
STACK OF WORDS ON ONE PAGE. IT DON'T MUSS
THINGS OR SCATTER INK BLOTS AROUND. OF COURSE
IT SAVES PAPER. . . . WORKING THE TYPE-WRITER RE-
MINDS ME OF OLD ROBERT BUCHANAN, WHO, YOU RE-
MEMBER, USED TO SET UP ARTICLES AT THE CASE
WITHOUT PREVIOUSLY PUTTING THEM IN THE FORM
OF MANUSCRIPT. I WAS LOST IN ADMIRATION FOR SUCH
MARVELOUS INTELLECTUAL CAPACITY. . . .

YOUR BROTHER

SAM [14]

And in March 1875, three months after he bought the machine, Twain was still willing to write a testimonial for the
Remington catalogue that, all things considered, can probably
be interpreted as an endorsement.

Gentlemen:
Please do not use my name in any way. Please do not even di-
vulge the fact that I own a machine. I have entirely stopped using the Type-Writer, for the reason that I never could write a
letter with it to anybody without receiving a request by return
mail that I would not only describe the machine but state what
progress I had made in the use of it, etc, etc. I don't like to write
letters, and so don't want people to know that I own this curiosity
breeding little joker.

Yours truly,
Saml L. Clemens [15]

A more significant customer than Mark Twain was the New
York firm of Dun, Barlow and Co. (the predecessor of Dun and
Bradstreet, Inc.). This company bought typewriters for its
home office, and then added forty more for its branch offices.
The machines were sent out complete with carbon paper,
tissue paper, and detailed instructions for typing reports and
returning them to the central file in the home office. According to Current, "previously subscribers to the credit-rating ser-

vices of the company had had to go to one of the offices and consult the handwritten ledger there. Now they could obtain by mail the data they required."[16] Dun, Barlow and Co. were slightly ahead of the times. Although typewriters were sold in the 1870s, they were not as popular as their producers had hoped. One reason for this is that in the 1870s typewriters still contained kinks that made them rather difficult and slow to operate. To many firms the new machine probably seemed more of an expense than an asset. Furthermore, there was some resistance to typewriting on the grounds of etiquette, as evidenced by the reply to a typed note that a Texas insurance man received from an agent: "I do not think it necessary then, nor will it be in the future, to have your letters to me taken to the printers' and set up like a handbill. I will be able to read your writing, and I am deeply chagrined to think you thought such a course necessary."[17]

But as the 1880s progressed, the typewriter became a more firmly established piece of office equipment. As the *Penman's Art Journal* observed in 1887, "Five years ago the typewriter was simply a mechanical curiosity. Today its monotonous click can be heard in almost every well regulated business establishment in the country. A great revolution is taking place, and the type writer is at the bottom of it."[18] Demand for the typewriter expanded so rapidly that supply could not keep up with it. In 1886 all typewriter factories combined were producing 15,000 machines a year. Two years later production had expanded to the point where Remington alone was manufacturing more than 1,500 a month, and the demand was still so great that foreign sales were temporarily ignored in favor of the domestic market. Once it caught on, the typewriter rapidly became a permanent office fixture.

It is clear that in the development of the typewriter, changes in the organization of capitalism gave rise to technological innovation, rather than the reverse. Inventors had been experimenting with writing machines for over 150 years before the Remington company started mass production of the Sholes typewriter. It was only in the 1870s, with the first indications of the expansion of offices and the growth of office work, that any capitalist firm was willing to invest in the manufacture of writing machines. It was not until the 1880s, when offices grew by leaps and bounds, that the typewriter began to sell. Rather than causing change, the typewriter followed in the wake of basic alterations in capitalism. Nonetheless, the typewriter did facilitate certain changes in office work. It aided in meeting the vastly increased demand in correspondence and record keeping, and in processing paper more quickly, for it *was* faster than handwriting. In addition, as will be discussed in the next chapter, it facilitated the employment of women as clerical workers, although again changes in the organization of capitalism were basically responsible for bringing them into offices.

Finally, the typewriter aided in the development of more rigid hierarchical structures within the office and in the diminution of what upward mobility existed in clerical work. Since the typewriter was most efficiently operated by a trained typist, the establishment of the job category "typist" followed almost immediately upon the typewriter itself. Those who started out as typists often remained typists for years. To be sure, this lack of upward mobility was a fate shared by some antebellum clerks and copyists. But the fact that the ability to type was a physical skill lent credence to the claim that a skilled typist was best suited only to the operation of the machine, and was not as useful for other kinds of office work. However, the typewriter at most only facilitated the development of hierarchical structures within the office; the root of that development lay in the reorganization of the office.

The Growth of Hierarchy

As firms grew, it was no longer possible for the capitalist or his top managers to personally oversee daily business operations.

They had to delegate tasks to lesser managers. The larger a firm became, the greater the number of middle- or low-level managers, and the more complex the structure of authority. It did not do to have this authority meted out in a haphazard manner. Rather, the well-designed bureaucratic hierarchy needed clear delineations of power and responsibility. At the bottom of this pyramid, of course, was the clerical worker.[19] The increasing division of labor itself reinforced the usefulness and necessity of hierarchical structures. A clerical worker who executed and understood only a small section of a firm's operations would not have the knowledge necessary to make a decision about problems that were not in his or her immediate purview. Broader understanding resided either with the clerical worker's immediate superior or with someone further up the hierarchical pyramid.

The case history of one advertising firm illustrates this interrelated process of the division of labor and of hierarchical structures of authority. It is not surprising that one of the few business case histories focusing on office operations is that of an advertising agency, for paperwork was the very product of an ad agency and the office the locus of production.

The Ayer Advertising Agency, N. W. Ayer and Son, was founded in Philadelphia in 1869.[20] F. W. Ayer founded it essentially as a one-man operation. (His father, who was a partner in the business and after whom the agency was named, was too sick to contribute much of anything.) By 1876 there were thirteen employees working in three main divisions. The Business Department solicited advertisements from various firms; the Forwarding Department placed advertisements in newspapers; and the Registry Department did the bookkeeping, made certain that advertisements had indeed been published as promised, and paid the bills. Four years later Ayer's increased its staff to forty-three and initiated "what was evidently the first attempt to make a systematic arrangement of the agency's work, extending the principle of functional division which had already been instituted." New departments

were created. The Bookkeeping Department kept the accounts; the Annual Department published the *American Newspaper Annual*, a sourcebook about newspapers; the Business
Advertising Department promoted Ayer's itself; and a separate
division was established to handle the business for religious
weeklies. Finally, the Merchandise Department handled the
anachronistic practice of remuneration in kind: some pub-
lishers were paid with materials such as ink and type, and
Ayer's accepted some payments in the form of books, patent
medicines, and other material from customers. There were
eight departments for forty-three employees, or about five employees per department, which seems an excessive subdivision. It suggests that the owners anticipated relatively rapid
growth.

They were not to be disappointed, for by 1900 Ayer's boasted
a staff of 163. Possibly its owners and managers were prompted
to reorganize by the example of larger firms that were institut-
ing similar subdivisions: the idea that a properly run business
should be divided into functionally defined departments was
no doubt beginning to take hold by this time.[21] Although Ayer's
hagiographer does not assess the effect of the 1880 reorganization on specific categories of clerical workers, it seems
likely that clerks were deprived of the opportunity to learn
about more than a relatively narrow aspect of the agency's operations. A clerk in the Bookkeeping Department might know
how to keep accounts, but next to nothing about how the Advertising Department went about soliciting business. Conversely, a clerk in Advertising might be capable of drafting attractive copy but know nothing about collecting overdue bills.

The division of labor at Ayer's did not stop with the creation
of departments. Jobs were also divided up within departments.
The Copy Department provides a clear example of this. It was
originally a part of the Business Department, and its personnel, who procured customers for Ayer's, also helped write advertising copy. After 1892, however, the firm began to hire
men who concentrated exclusively on writing ads: those who

were adept at drumming up business were often mediocre at writing copy, and vice versa. In 1900 the Copy Department was split off from the Business Department and became a department in its own right. Up to that point an individual copyman had been a jack-of-all-trades who wrote text, prepared ideas for illustrations, set up layouts, selected typefaces, and so forth. But in 1898 Ayer's hired a commercial artist to prepare layouts and finished drawings; four years later it added a specialist to buy engravings and finished artwork; in 1904 an illustrator was hired; and in 1910 an art director was brought on. By 1912 "the division of work in the preparation of copy was recognized in a formal way by organizing within the Copy Department an Editorial Bureau to write advertisements, an Art Bureau to take charge of all the art work, an Engraving Bureau to buy plates and other means of mechanical reproduction, and a Stenographic Bureau to handle the typing and correspondence of the Department."[22]

This further subdivision was not without its headaches. It "caused the same sort of difficulty that the multiplication of departments had previously caused the Ayer organization as a whole: between bureaus there were misunderstandings, delays, and confusion. To coordinate the work of the specialists a Production Bureau was created in 1916, followed by a Detail Bureau in 1917."[23] Hower notes this change with approval and goes on to remark that "creative workers were relieved of petty details and routine work, enabling them to work more effectively at their primary tasks. And, since the routine work could be done by comparatively unskilled employees, the ultimate result was better copy at lower cost."[24] The Ayer management may have undertaken department reorganization and a division of labor ostensibly for reasons of "rationality" and "efficiency," but the fact that such changes also lowered labor costs was not ignored.

The increasing division of labor at Ayer's developed concurrently with the growth of formal hierarchical structures. F. W. Ayer himself at first rejected the advice of his own managers, who had pressed for such innovations. His reluctance was not at all unusual. Many nineteenth-century capitalists who had built their firms from the ground up had a tendency to rely on older, more personal systems of management that younger executives found outmoded. In 1896 a group of Ayer's higher-level employees recommended that an executive be hired to coordinate and supervise the agency's work, a step that would clearly separate the "managerial function" from the day-to-day production of the agency. Ayer objected, arguing that the firm's past experience proved him right:

> Mr. Wallace undertook to be an executive head as to the management of an order. He did this with great skill and ability, *but the result was that everybody else became his assistant, and no one developed.* This method besides broke Mr. Wallace down, and there was no one to take his place. . . . The way to handle our business is to *cultivate responsibility and accountability in individuals.* . . . The great essential is that each [employee] should be faithful, dependable, and capable. . . . The executive man proposed would be sick sometimes, absent at others on vacation, etc. . . . *Perhaps the firm could have done more business and made more money with an executive man, but the others would all be pawns.*[25]

Ayer neglected to point out that he himself functioned as the firm's general manager. He understood all of the firm's operations and made it his business to know what was going on in all departments and to intervene as he saw fit.

By 1905, however, Ayer recognized that his one-man supervision no longer sufficed, and established five committees of three men each to oversee various aspects of the firm. This system of management held for a few years, but came in for criticism because the final authority for making decisions was not clearly delegated. And in 1911 and 1912 Ayer's was totally reorganized. The committees were discarded and a general manager was placed in charge of the entire staff. The general manager had the final authority for deciding major issues and formulating policy; he referred lesser decisions to his assistants; and so on down the line. This system had one great advantage: the power to make various decisions was now assigned to various levels of the hierarchy. Ideally there would no longer be confusion about who had the right to decide what. In 1912, in explaining this reorganization to his staff, Ayer showed that he had forsaken his earlier principles of the development and growth of each individual and adopted a new set of principles that stressed efficiency:

> Our business has suffered from its beginning from a fact for which none of you are accountable. The lack lay in me and in my failure to recognize it and remedy it early in the business history. I never had a day's business training in my life. My father never did. I went out of the school room into this business. . . . I lacked efficiency in the things which I undertook to do. I had to feel out and find a way for everything that I did. It was a great relief to me when I got a young man who could keep the books which I had been keeping evenings. I never experienced a greater sense of relief than I did when the exactness of those entries no longer depended on me, and so one after another of those departments of the work which involved detail have been let go of, but *not in a well defined way*, and the persons who took hold of them at times were no better fitted for them than I was or had not had the training any more than I had. And so our business came to be a collection of methods devised by ourselves the day it came up to be done. Now that isn't the best way to get the best methods or to get the most speed, or the most economical administration. Our business has, I think, always suffered, from that cause, and as a result of this laxity way back at the beginning.[26]

In his discussion, Hower does not mention the effect of the development of hierarchical structures at Ayer's on the firm's lower-level clerical employees. Nonetheless, it stands to reason that a system that carefully designated the powers and range of responsibilities of the higher-level employees would do the same for the clerical workers. In a situation where the lines of authority were defined poorly, if at all, it no doubt would be more possible for a clerical worker to decide for him or herself about matters that came up. In fact, Ayer's 1896 remarks indicate that independence was encouraged. But as lines of authority hardened and duties were more precisely spelled out, such initiatives on the part of clerical workers were likely to be discouraged. Ayer's management prided itself on its generous paternalism. This included such schemes as "premium time . . . to encourage punctuality, service bonuses . . . to foster loyalty, the savings funds and the Employees' Trust . . . to encourage thrift and attention to the work at hand."[27] But when it came to getting every last minute out of an employee's workday, the velvet glove came off to display the iron fist.

When Ayer's was just getting started in the 1870s, the work week was Monday through Saturday, from 8 A.M. to 6 P.M., with an hour off for lunch. By 1885 the firm made allowances for the heat of the Philadelphia summer and released its employees at 5 P.M., and at 4 P.M. on Saturdays. This demanding work schedule created problems and by 1886 management expressed concern over tardiness:

> [The firm] had attempted for a time to encourage punctuality by special citations of the employees who had not been late during each month. The bestowal of praise was apparently not effective, and the firm now gave notice that time lost through unexcused lateness would be taken from holiday periods or its equivalent deducted from the weekly wages. *This feature is especially interesting in view of the fact that the employees were not paid for the overtime which they often had to work.* To take the sting out of this rule a scheme of rewards for punctuality was announced: every employee would be granted one half-holiday each month, provided that he had had not more than ten unexcused latenesses during the preceding month.[28]

This carrot-and-stick policy still was not completely successful. Management continued to complain that workers fudged time-slips and produced questionable excuses for lateness.

The work hours at Ayer's were not substantially reduced. In

1892 employees voted to take only a half-hour lunch on Friday and Saturday, so that they might leave an hour earlier on Saturday throughout the year. In 1899, however, Ayer's got the contract for the National Biscuit Company (Uneeda Biscuit), and management decided the added business meant that they could no longer afford to shorten the Saturday workday in the summer. They announced this decision in the following notice:

To Our Employees:

re EARLY CLOSING.

We have approached this question this year with great misgiving, for the reason that we have been unable to see how the work now in hand can be promptly done in reduced hours. It must be apparent to every one that we are now unusually loaded for this time of year. The nature of the work is also somewhat peculiar, that is to say, with it we are being placed on trial by new clients whose dispositon to give us further business will be affected by the expedition and ability with which we handle the business we now have in hand.

The business feeds us all. To shorten our working hours, therefore, at the expense of slighting or delaying our work would be to injure every one of us—employees and employers alike. (Speaking of injury, let us also be careful that no one is hurt in the halls and stairways in rushes such as have recently followed the closing gong.)

In view of present conditions, we have thought the following the best arrangement for this season—to close at four o'clock Saturdays and five o'clock other days, but to shorten the lunch period to one-half hour every day. This schedule to go in effect Saturday, July 1st, and terminate Saturday, September 2nd, 1899.

It must also be kept in mind that vacations are to be taken during this same period. We, therefore, ask every employee to see not only that his or her own work not fall behind, but also to be watchful and helpful in all the work of the department, working after five o'clok or at other hours whenever the welfare of the business demands it.

June 30, 1899 [29]

Shortly thereafter Ayer's management began to relent, if somewhat grudgingly. In 1902 the work week was shortened from fifty-four to fifty-one hours, and the year-round closing time was advanced from 6 to 5:30 P.M. Nonetheless, when announcing this policy, management made it clear that it wanted no liberties taken.

> Our idea in doing this (which, on the present pay-roll basis, would cost us over $5,000 per year) is to enable you to get out on the street before the six o'clock trolley rush, and also enable this to be done without a crowd about the elevators. We would make the lunch period one hour every day instead of four days as heretofore. This will allow ample time to get up and down the elevators at noon without confusion.
>
> We are quite willing to try this new order of things *on one condition, namely, that you will work until 5:30 o'clock, taking after that hour whatever time you may wish to wash up, put on hats and wraps, and leave the building in an orderly manner.*[30]

Over the next thirty years the hours were gradually reduced until, in 1932, they were shortened to thirty-five hours a week and the office was completely closed on Saturdays.

One feature stands out in this account of the organization of working hours at Ayer's: management was primarily interested in "the welfare of the business," despite occasional references to the well-being of its employees ("The business feeds us all," and so on). Ayer's may have liked to see itself in the complimentary light of benevolent paternalism, but, in the final analysis, it was mainly interested in extracting maximal effort from its workers. The managers who wrote the notices to employees were a far cry from the 1850s lawyer in Melville's "Bartleby," who was so ambivalent about his position as an employer that he let the clerk Bartleby literally drive him from his office. By the late nineteenth century, the rhetoric of paternalism was still in the air in the larger offices, but relations between employer and employee had ceased to be very personal. Instead, they had become regulated and relatively impersonal:

Melville's "Turkey," who returned from lunch too drunk to do any useful work, would hardly be tolerated in an office where clerical workers were expressly instructed not to don their hats and coats on company time. The personal harshness or benevolence of an individual employer was being replaced by rules that were less subject to daily interpretation or modification, even though they had originally been laid down by individual owners and managers.

The Ayer management was fond of citing opportunities for advancement within the firm as reason why employees should consider the welfare of the business identical with their own. Hower, who served as a sort of court biographer to Ayer's, spoke approvingly of such opportunities: "Men have risen from errand-boy jobs to department headship, and, since incorporation, to presidency. The firm has always promoted from within rather than hired executives from outside, and for over twenty-five years there has been no significant departure from this policy."[31] This rosy picture of promotions within Ayer's was at least partially true in the company's early years, when there were relatively few employees. "Judging by their weekly wages," Hower argues, "we must conclude that most of the [employees] hired in the 'seventies began as clerks or office boys and learned the business from the bottom rung of the ladder."[32] This is borne out by a letter that F. W. Ayer wrote to his uncle in 1873:

July 28, 1873
Philadelphia.

Dear Uncle Geo.

I expect to make some changes in our office help this fall and wish to find a fairly educated boy of about 16 to 18 smart as a steel trap and thoroughly reliable. He must come determined to learn our business and grow up with us and if he comes in that way we can give him in my opinion as fine a chance as could be desired. He must be willing to work early and late and for one interest. Don't want any boy who has to have everything told him but one who *sees* what needs to be done and does it. How would

Aunt Laura's Charlie suit me? Would she wish him to leave
home, would he do as I told him and could I depend upon his
staying right along at a fair price? [33]

But there is good reason to believe that as the firm grew in
the 1880s and 1890s and thereafter, the chance of a low-level
clerical worker eventually rising to a partnership became extremely remote. First of all, the firm soon began to hire those
who were already trained for specific jobs. Thus, Ayer's hired
an experienced bookkeeper in 1877; a man with twenty years
general experience in business in 1883; a stenographer in
1886; and a commercial artist in 1898. [34] While some of these
employees might be promoted, the promotions would probably
not go beyond the headship of a particular bureau or department. Hower tacitly admits that the practice of promoting out
of the ranks all the way to the top was on its way out, and con-
sciously discouraged by the Ayer's management, in the 1930s:

> As the Ayer firm has grown, one problem of promotion has emerged
> which presents special interest and difficulty. The Ayer manage-
> ment, following general business practice, has tended to promote
> to general executive positions men who distinguished themselves
> as field representatives, copywriters, plans men or other special-
> ists of the agency business. Sometimes, as a result, *men who were
> essentially expert advertising technicians were placed in posi-
> tions requiring a high degree of talent for general business admin-
> istration.* Occasionally one of them was able to adapt himself to
> the new situation, but in many instances the firm deprived itself of
> a good technician without gaining a capable administrator. In re-
> cent years the Ayer firm has begun to appreciate the distinction
> between advertising expert and a general business executive, and
> has endeavored to obtain more of the latter type. This development
> is, of course, in harmony with the general tendency of business
> to exercise more discernment in assigning employees to spe-
> cific jobs. [35]

Furthermore, it was one thing for an "expert advertising
technician" to be promoted to a general executive position and

quite another for a clerical worker to be given such a promotion. The trend at Ayer's toward hiring specialized workers to fill specific posts, with slim chance of indefinite promotion, was clearly more apparent among lower-level clerical workers. Although it is not certain that all of the latter were women, a sizable and growing proportion of them probably were. Hower has this to say about the status of women at Ayer's:

> The positions held by women in N. W. Ayer and Son have been almost exclusively clerical or stenographic. It is worthy of note, however, that in every division of the agency, with the exception of the Printing Department, women have been advanced to positions involving considerable responsibility and judgment. For many years one woman has been cashier of the firm, and recently another was made secretary of the corporation.[36]

Neither of the specific jobs that Hower mentions could truly be called executive positions. Two positions of relative authority do not amount to much when one considers that Ayer's employed forty women in 1890, out of a total of 109 employees; 108 in 1915, out of 264; and 417 in 1932, out of 906. It may be assumed that most of these women worked as typists, stenographers, and other low-level clerical workers, and that it was rare for any of them to get a substantial promotion.

Possibly there was a certain amount of upward mobility among clerical workers in Ayer's early years, although it is significant that the single example of potential upward mobility Hower offers is one in which the office boy for whom a bright future is held out turns out to be a relative of the firm's owners. It seems clear that as Ayer's expanded, the chances for a clerical worker to rise within the firm became increasingly slim, and the talk of "opportunities for advancement" applied largely to men who started off in relatively advanced positions. Expansion at Ayer's produced a host of new "middle-management" jobs, as well as many more clerical positions. But judging from Hower's account, the more rewarding jobs within the hierarchy—such as copy-writing, accounting, or supervisory positions—went to men. Women were restricted to the clerical work at the bottom of the hierarchy.

This short history of the Ayer advertising agency illustrates several developments that began to show up in offices after the Civil War. First of all, an extension of the division of labor resulted not only in the reorganization of firms into functionally defined departments, but also in the division of clerical work within those departments. Both this extension of the division of labor and the sheer growth in size of offices encouraged the development of hierarchical structures of authority. No longer did individual owners and managers personally oversee and make decisions about all aspects of office work. Instead, the authority to make decisions was delegated through a hierarchical structure, and policies that had heretofore been left to the discretion of an individual were codified. This state of affairs was reinforced by the fact that the division of labor had already deprived clerical workers of the information and understanding of the office's operations that would have enabled them to make decisions on their own. The paternalism of the pre–Civil War office, be it strict or generous, was on the wane. Finally, opportunities for a clerical worker to advance to ownership or management positions were greatly diminished.

4

Women Enter the Office

During the Civil War the U.S. Treasurer General, Francis Elias Spinner, confronted a severe labor shortage caused by the large numbers of men in Union uniforms.[1] He decided over considerable opposition to hire some female clerks, who worked at relatively mechanical tasks such as sorting and packaging bonds and currency.[2] This "experiment" was continued after the war and in 1869 Spinner declared "'upon his word' that it had been a complete success: 'Some of the females doing more and better work for $900 per annum than many male clerks who were paid double that amount.'"[3] Such wage figures indicate one of the reasons Spinner thought so highly of his experiment: female labor was cheaper than male. A contemporary claimed that most of these early female clerks got their positions through political patronage, with the result that some of them were not well trained for their jobs and had to take writing lessons after they were employed.[4] But a study of federal government clerks from 1862 to 1890 has found that, by and large, the women did have sufficient education for clerical work, most of them having remained in school at least until the age of sixteen. They came overwhelmingly from white, native-born, middle-class families and were the daughters of men with jobs that ranged from clerks to judges; almost none of them were the daughters of craftsmen, much less unskilled laborers. Whether they were single, widowed, or, less frequently, married, these women sought clerical jobs out of economic necessity. Many needed the income to help support their families or pay off large debts. Others worked to maintain their families' middle-class standard of living—one widow, for example, needed the money to buy Latin and Greek books so that her son could prepare for Princeton.[5]

Although these government employees are often regarded as the first female clerks, women also found employment in other urban offices. In Washington some copied speeches and other documents for members of Congress, and in other cities they worked for lawyers. A book called *How Women Can Make Money* by Virginia Penny advised women to group together to rent an office in the business section of a city from which they could hire out their copying services for three to four cents for every hundred words. Women also worked as stenographers, although a New York court stenographer in 1869 claimed that, even though there were openings for women in stenography, "phonographic reporting [was work] in which the pay is remunerative, but into which [women] do not seem inclined to enter." By the 1860s there were also female bookkeepers and accountants. An article in the suffrage newspaper the *Revolution* claimed that a merchant in New York had replaced his $1,800 a year male bookkeeper with a woman earning $500 a year.[6]

Feminization proceeded at different rates in different job categories. It proceeded briskly among stenographers and typists: by 1880 women already made up 40 percent of the group; by 1900 they accounted for over three-fourths; and in 1930 they completely dominated the field—over 95 percent. The case was different for bookkeepers, cashiers and accountants. Women made up less than 6 percent of this group in 1880. That figure had only increased to 29 percent by 1900, and by 1930, was still only slightly more than half. Among messenger, errand, and office boys and girls, females never outnumbered males. The number of women employed in this category lagged far behind the other groups, and after 1920 the entire category declined, probably as a result of the growing use of the telephone. The largest group of clerical workers, clerks, was still more male than female in 1930, when the percentage of women stood at 35 percent. There were almost as many female clerks as there were female stenographers and typists in 1930, but because the category "stenographers and typists" contained less than half as many people, women were much more dominant in it.

The process of feminization that shows up in these aggregate statistics for the United States is also reflected in the employment history of a single firm. During the first five years of the Ayer advertising agency, no women were employed. In 1874 a woman was hired for a few months, and in 1876 the first two permanent female employees started work. Female employment at Ayer's then grew quite rapidly, for by 1890, 36.7 percent of the 109 employees were women. For the next forty years the percentage of women at Ayer's hovered around 40 percent, reaching 46 percent in 1932. The jobs these women did were "almost exclusively clerical or stenographic."[7]

The feminization of clerical work did not happen overnight. The demand for clerical workers in the United States in the late nineteenth and the early twentieth centuries was so great that both men and women poured into clerical posts. But the trend was for women to take over an increasing percentage of clerical jobs. The feminization of stenographers and typists was markedly more rapid than that of other categories. This may have been because such jobs seemed new and different from those that had existed in the pre–Civil War office. They had never been defined as "men's work" and women thus entered them with relative ease.

The Role of the Typewriter

One of the ways women entered clerical work was by mastering the typewriter and then finding a job as a typist.[8] When Mark Twain bought his first typewriter in early 1875, the salesman had a "type girl" on hand to demonstrate the machine to prospective customers.[9] And in late 1875 this ad for the Remington typewriter appeared in the *Nation*:

CHRISTMAS PRESENT
for a boy or girl

And the benevolent can, by the gift of a "Type-Writer" to a poor, deserving young woman, put her at once in the way of earning a good living as a copyist or corresponding clerk.

No invention has opened for women so broad and easy an avenue to profitable and suitable employment as the "Type-Writer," and it merits the careful consideration of all thoughtful and charitable persons interested in the subject of work for woman.

Mere girls are now earning from $10 to $20 per week with the "Type-Writer," and we can at once secure good situations for one hundred expert writers on it in court-rooms in this city.

The public is cordially invited to call and inspect the working of the machine, and obtain all information at our show-rooms.[10]

But in 1875 and for a few years thereafter, the typewriter was still thought of as a frill by most businessmen. It was not until the 1880s that typewriters were manufactured and sold in large numbers.

In the 1880s, also, the employment of women in offices began to climb sharply (see Appendix, Table 1.). This coincidence has led some analysts to conclude that the invention of the typewriter was basically responsible for the employment of women in offices in the United States. For example, a pamphlet put out by the Women's Bureau of the United States Department of Labor asserts that "not only . . . has the typewriter revolutionized modern business methods but it has *created* an occupation calling for more women than have been employed as a result of any other invention."[11] Bruce Bliven, the author of a history of the typewriter, recounts the story of how the New York YWCA started training young women typists in 1881. Far from succumbing to mental and physical breakdowns under the strain of their new occupation, as some observers had warned, these women quickly found jobs. The YWCA was soon deluged with many more requests for typists than it could fill. Bliven concludes that "the revolution came rather quietly, on high-buttoned shoes, accompanied not by gunfire or bombs bursting in air, but by a considerable amount of rather obnoxious snickering." [12]

Just as it would be a mistake to say that the typewriter was responsible for the growth of offices after the Civil War, so would it be erroneous to credit it with the employment of women in those offices. The figures in Table 1 (see Appendix) show that female employment was increasing rapidly throughout the clerical occupations, and not just among stenographers and typists.

Although the typewriter was not responsible for the employment of women as clerical workers, its existence probably facilitated or eased the entrance of women into offices. It was such a new machine that it had not been "sex-typed" as masculine. Thus women who worked as typists did not face the argument that a typewriter was a machine fit only for men. In fact, it was not too long afterwards that women were claimed to be more manually dexterous and tolerant of routine than men and therefore more suited, by virtue of their very natures, to operate typewriters.

Causes of Feminization

Changes in the structure of capitalism in the United States brought women into offices. The expansion and consolidation of capitalist firms after the Civil War caused a rapid increase in the amount of correspondence and record keeping required by those firms. This in turn resulted in the growth of offices and an immediate increase in the need for clerical workers. That, in short, explains the demand. Where was the supply to come from?

The basic skill required of clerical workers was literacy. The supply therefore had to come from those segments of the population that had some education, and at this time women, as well as men, had advanced schooling. In fact, as Table 2 shows (see Appendix), the number of women high school graduates exceeded that of men during the last decades of the nineteenth century.

And women's labor was cheaper than men's. Patriarchal social relations devalued the labor of women compared to that of men from similar backgrounds. The reasons for this are legion. First of all, there was the widespread belief that women were simply, and by the very nature of things, inferior to men. In addition, women were often thought to be working for "pin money" with which to make frivolous purchases. Since they were not thought to be supporting themselves or their families, there was nothing the matter with paying them low wages. Then there was the argument that women were not serious members of the labor force: they would be returning to an exclusively domestic life either as soon as they married or, at the very latest, as soon as they bore children. Such transient workers did not deserve the higher wage with which an employer might try to attract and keep a more steadfast male worker. Finally, women's depressed wages did drive them back into the home, where they again became available to fill a subordinate position within the domestic division of labor. Whether or not this worked to the ultimate benefit of men, it certainly provided them with short-term benefits.[13]

On the face of it, the cheapness of labor ought to explain why employers preferred women over men. But women's labor in the United States has always come cheaper than men's, so that it is not immediately obvious why employers did not always show preference for females. There must be a further reason why employers started to favor women for certain clerical positions.

The supply of literate male labor was simply not large enough to fill the great demand for office workers. The expansion of capitalist firms created not only a much larger need for clerical workers, but also an increased demand for managerial personnel. As is clear from the discussion of the proliferation of hierarchical structures within late nineteenth-century firms, the managerial corps necessitated by this new system of finely delegated authority expanded mightily. An educated man, faced with the choice among positions within the office hierarchy, was unlikely to choose to be a typist instead of a manager, who was higher-paid and invested with a fair degree of authority and power. The expansion of capitalist firms, coupled with the growth of cities at the end of the nineteenth century, also led to a rise in the number of jobs ancillary to business operations. Lawyers are an excellent example: in 1870 there were 40,736 lawyers in the United States, all but five of whom were men. By 1900 there were almost three times as many lawyers, 114,640, over 99 percent of whom were men. There had been one lawyer for every 307 people employed in all occupations in the United States in 1870; by 1900 there was one lawyer for every 254 such persons.[14] Thus a man who had enough education and literacy skills (the ability to spell reasonably well, to write a legible hand, to do basic arithmetic accurately) to obtain a job as a clerical worker was also probably educated enough to at least aspire to, and in many cases to attain, a managerial or professional position. As a consequence, the supply of men available for clerical work was considerably diminished.

Furthermore, fewer boys than girls were graduating from high school in the United States (see Appendix, Table 2). If high school and college graduations are considered together, more men than women were receiving secondary school diplomas or better during the years 1870 and 1880. But in 1890 and 1900, the number of women receiving high school diplomas or better had outstripped the number of men. Despite the fact that consistently far more men than women graduated from college, the number of women finishing high school grew to so outweigh the number of men that the surplus of male over female college graduates was cancelled out. In addition, the men who were reaching those high educational levels were likely to be supplying the demand for managers and professionals. Thus the demand for managers and professionals and the fact that more women than men were reaching relatively high levels of formal education combine to explain why it was that the ever-increasing demand for clerical workers was met by women.

Other factors, though secondary, also influenced feminization. First of all, the employment of women as clerks in the United States Treasury Department during the Civil War established a precedent that may have eased the entrance of women into offices ten and fifteen years later. The employment of female clerks in the Treasury Department showed that it was possible for women to work in offices. Women had gotten a toe in the office door. As a result, when structural changes in capitalism produced a dramatic rise in the demand for clerical workers, it was slightly easier for women to push the door wide open.

A second factor that facilitated—as opposed to caused—the employment of women was the invention and production of the typewriter. Women were employed in increasing numbers throughout the entire gamut of clerical occupations, and not just as typists. The process that underlay the employment of women in offices was similar to that which underlay the successful manufacture of a typewriter in the first place—the expansion and consolidation of capitalist firms. But the fact that the typewriter was sex-neutral, without historical ties to workers of either sex, meant that female typists did not have to meet the argument that they were operating a man's machine.

Finally, the reorganization of the division of labor within the office may have abetted its feminization. It is possible that if offices had simply expanded without being reorganized, women would have had a more difficult time entering clerical work. The reorganization of many offices often resulted in a redivision of clerical labor and in the creation of new jobs, from stenographers and typists to file clerks, billing clerks, and the like. Since many of these jobs, or at least their labels, had not existed before the growth of the office, they were not defined as men's jobs. Women who took such positions did not face the argument that they were taking over men's work.

Nonetheless, the roots of the feminization of clerical work lay in political-economic conditions that were independent of the job itself. Changes in the structure of capitalism caused a rapid increase in the demand for clerical workers, a demand that was met in part by an available supply of literate women. Furthermore, it seems that many employers were only too glad to employ female labor in place of more costly male labor. The feminization of clerical work was not intrinsic to the job itself, despite ideological justifications that arose after the fact. By its very nature, clerical work was neither men's work nor women's work.

Clerical jobs were available to women, but, for feminization to occur, women had to be available to take the jobs. A variety of factors produced a supply of women to fill the demand. The economic decline of small, family-owned farms and businesses frequently forced daughters into the labor force. Clerical work was generally seen as more desirable than industrial work, and this spurred women of working-class origins to seek clerical jobs. Productive work in the home was on the decline, making the labor of both working-class and non-working-class women available for jobs outside the domestic sphere. And clerical work was one of the few options for literate women seeking jobs that required literate workers.

Ever since 1820, the proportion of the United States labor force made up of farmers had been declining. In 1820 farmers constituted fully three-quarters of the nation's labor force. By 1880 that proportion had already been reduced to one-half, and by 1949 it was down to one-eighth.[15] If farm laborers are excluded from the calculations, the proportion of the gainfully employed population on small farms shrinks even more. Be-

tween 1870 and 1890 that proportion hovered around 24 percent but then fell steadily and by 1930 amounted to only 12
percent. (See Appendix, Table 3.) The death blow to the small,
independent farmer as a significant member of and influence
on the class structure of the United States was dealt in the
1920s and 1930s by a prolonged fall in farm prices. Since then,
farming in the United States has been dominated by large capitalists. The proportion of farm owners shrank, many farmers
being forced to mortgage their property or, worse yet, to de-
fault on their mortgages and lose their land altogether.

Some farm families were literally driven off the land, leaving behind their heavily mortgaged farms to be sold by the
banks to large capitalist farmers and companies. In less desperate families, the departure from the land would often take
place from one generation to the next. Sons and daughters
who were loath to commit themselves to lives of hard physical
toil for diminishing rewards would choose to move to a city,
where they became part of the urban labor force.

Although the decline of the small, independent farmer as a
class had hardly begun in earnest, by the end of the nineteenth century the large cities of the East were already beginning to feel the effects. The new homesteads of the West absorbed only some of the eastern farmers forced off their land.
Others who found they could no longer make ends meet were
already moving into the cities in the waning years of the nineteenth century, although it was not until the twentieth that
displaced small farmers really began to swell the urban labor
force. The ranks of clerical workers included people of small-
farm origins from the outset.

The situation of small-business proprietors differed significantly from that of farmers. From 1870 to 1930 they not only
held their own numerically and as a proportion of the labor
force but, in fact, grew.[16] Although the class as a whole maintained itself through the years, however, individual members
of the classic petite bourgeoisie did not always manage to

make ends meet, much less prosper. Thousands of fledgling businesses were started by hopeful entrepreneurs; almost as many failed.[17]

These small entrepreneurs lived in constant dread of failure and imposed long hours on themselves and their families in order to fend off financial disaster. "But the average life of these old middle-class, especially urban, units in the twentieth century is short; the coincidence of family unit and work-situation among the old middle class is a pre-industrial fact. So even as the centralization of property contracts their 'independence,' it liberates the children of the old middle class's smaller entrepreneurs."[18]

Some of those children were "liberated" to become clerical workers. The endemic financial insecurity of many small businessmen often meant not only that their children were reluctant to follow them in an unstable occupation, but also, in many cases, that the children were forced to support themselves. Thus the classic petite bourgeoisie contributed to the pool of people available for work in offices.

Booth Tarkington's novel *Alice Adams*, published in 1921, portrays a woman pushed into the clerical labor force by her family's financial plight. Alice Adams is a young woman in a mid-western city from a minor manager's family who would like nothing better than to be included in the social life of the city's bourgeoisie. For a time some of the upper-class girls are rather friendly to Alice and invite her to dinner parties and dances. After a while, however, they begin to snub her and finally dismiss her from their lives for being too "pushy." Alice's father had started out as a clerk for J. A. Lamb, one of the city's leading businessmen, and gradually worked himself up to the position of manager of the sundries department. There he works for many a faithful year until a stroke forces him into a long convalescence. While he is recuperating, his wife urges him to leave his job and set up a business of his own, so that they can make enough money to buy his daughter the "nice things"—more clothes, a better house in a better neighbor-hood—that Alice's mother thinks she should be enjoying. Vir-gil Adams would be quite happy to return to his position at Lamb's and feels that he was both a valued member of the staff and financially secure. But his wife employs a constant bar-rage of emotional blackmail until he gives in, raises some capi-tal by mortgaging his house, and opens a glue factory.

The story of how Virgil Adams learned the formula for this wonderful glue bears on the outcome of the drama. When Adams was a young clerk working at Lamb's, J. A. Lamb set him and another clerk to inventing a glue that would really stick. But by the time they had succeeded, Lamb had lost in-terest in branching into glue manufacture. The other clerk died, leaving Virgil with the formula for the glue, which he kept in his head. From time to time he would try to reinterest Lamb in investing in a glue factory, but never with any suc-cess. When his wife finally persuades him to go on his own, Adams balks because he feels that the formula belongs to J. A. Lamb at least as much as to him. But in the end he swallows his scruples, quits his position at Lamb's, and starts to make glue. Lamb retaliates by starting his own glue factory, which, given the much greater amount of capital available to him, is bound to drive Adams out of business. Recognizing his inev-itable defeat, Adams rages at Lamb, suffers another stroke, and becomes so ill that his doctor advises him never to work again. The Adams family is now left in such financial straits that Mrs. Adams has to take in boarders. For her part, Alice faces her true economic position squarely and sets out to be-come a working woman:

> She passed the tobacconist's, and before her was that dark en-trance to the wooden stairway leading up to Frincke's Business College—the very doorway she had always looked upon as the end of youth and the end of hope.
>
> How often she had gone by there, hating the dreary obscurity of that stairway; how often she had thought of this obscurity as something lying in wait to obliterate the footsteps of any girl who

should ascend into the smoky darkness above! Never had she passed without those ominous imaginings of hers: pretty girls turning into old maids "taking dictation"—old maids of a dozen different types, yet all looking a little like herself.

Well, she was here at last! She looked up and down the street quickly, and then, with a little heave of the shoulders, she went bravely in, under the sign, and began to climb the wooden steps. Half-way up the shadows were heaviest, but after that the place began to seem brighter. There was an open window overhead somewhere, she found, and the steps at the top were gay with sunshine.[19]

This is a rather saccharine ending to a novel that is otherwise a fairly relentless picture of the dynamics of the class structure in an early twentieth-century city. Alice Adams's story graphically illustrates the political-economic situation of her times: Virgil Adams, starting out as a clerk, worked his way up to a lower-level management position, and then lost all his financial security when he tried to enter the ranks of independent businessmen. The desperate financial plight of her family obliged the daughter to relinquish her fantasies of joining the bourgeoisie and to become a clerical worker. *Alice Adams* is a clear case of the process by which the instability of small-business families contributed to the pool of potential clerical workers. A study of Washington government clerks has found that many middle-class women sought clerical jobs when their families fell on financial hard times. A woman in 1881 explained that she was applying for a job because "a few years ago I enjoyed all the luxuries of an elegant home, but commercial disaster, which as you know has ruined so many men, compels me now to seek assistance from strangers."[20]

For an Alice Adams, working for wages was a new experience. For many daughters of working-class families, however, membership in the labor force was nothing new. The vast majority of working-class families were unable to afford the luxury of keeping out of the labor force an unmarried daughter whose labor was not essential to the maintenance of the home.

Single working-class women were expected to enter the labor force as a matter of course. In fact, a writer in 1929 considered it a sign of the improved condition of the working class that its children were staying in school longer and longer, rather than entering the labor force out of economic necessity:

> The rising standard of living of manual workers has made it possible for more of them to provide their children with the high-school education necessary to clerical positions, and the popular belief in education as the open sesame to opportunity has been an incentive to increased high school attendance. This increase in the high school population—the rate of which, within the last thirty years, has been about twenty times the rate of the increase in the population—has thrown upon the vocational market thousands of girls with a high school education, a large proportion of whom aspire to clerical positons.[21]

The main reason working-class girls "aspired" to clerical work was that it paid better than most jobs open to women. In 1883, at the very beginning of the influx of large numbers of women into clerical work, female office workers in Boston were relatively well off compared to women in other working-class occupations. Copyists in personal service earned an average weekly wage of $6.78, bookkeepers earned $6.55, cashiers earned $7.43, and clerks (it is not clear from the available information whether "clerks" refers to clerks in offices or stores, or both) earned $5.28. Although a highly skilled craft-worker in manufacturing, such as a button-hole-maker for men's shirts, could earn as much as $10.00, most women working in manufacturing did not make over $5.00, and some made considerably less.[22] These wages do not take into account the shorter hours women in offices enjoyed, a factor that would make their average hourly wage even better when compared to that of other working-class women. In 1910 a study of the incomes and expenditures of 450 Boston working women found that clerical work was second only to professional occupations in annual net income.[23]

In addition to better wages, clerical work brought higher

status than many other "female" occupations, such as factory
work, domestic service, and clerking in stores. The argument
has been made that this higher status was a result of a cleaner
work environment, shorter hours, such benefits as vacation
and sick leave, and the notion that clerical work could lead
to promotions of some importance in the business world.[24]
Whether or not such analyses are correct, the fact that clerical
work enjoyed higher status does not seem to be in question.
The following case histories show that at least some working-
class women saw clerical work not only as more prestigious,
but even as a means of rising out of the working class itself.

Maimie Pomerantz Jacobs worked at various periods as a
prostitute in Philadelphia. Through a social welfare agency
she was put in touch with a wealthy Boston matron, Fanny
Quincy Howe, who befriended her as a kind of good-works
project. Their friendship was carried on mainly by mail and a
voluminous correspondence was built over the years.[25] From
May 1912 to 1914, Maimie worked as a secretary, but left in dis-
gust because of the constant surveillance of her superiors.
While training for the position, however, she had been very
hopeful about the changes it would bring, or at least wanted to
give Mrs. Howe an optimistic impression. Maimie wrote the
following letter to Mrs. Howe while she was enrolled in a business school:

Philadelphia
December 13, 1911

In School

My Dear Friend,

I must tell you first how happy I am. I want to write you about
something else and then tell you about the school but I am so
enthusiastic, that I will tell you first about the school. Since I
realized what I missed by not having any childhood and necessarily no education, I have wished it possible for me to take up
something, in fact most anything but now I feel this is the beginning of a new era for I am not only being educated in a sense (for

we take English here and now I will know about moods and ten-
ses etc.) but it will be the means of my being above living ques-
tionably or accepting favors. When I walk around town now I am
a different person—for my future looms up large. It is a question
with me why I did not do this long ago, for certainly at various
times I have had large sums of money that would have amply
paid for the lessons but my life being such an irregular one, my
desires were not the same as now. I had ambitious thoughts but
they would come and go—for I had no one to help me. I did not
have anyone that cared whether I earned my living one way or
the other and I lacked sufficient back bone to want to do things
just for myself. It's all different now though and I no more think
of doing wrong than you.[26]

A short story, "Sarah and Mr. Salamovitch," published in
1907, provides another illustration of the hopes that were
pinned on clerical work. Sarah was the daughter of a Jewish
immigrant family who came to the United States from Russia
when she was ten. Her parents had worked hard, her mother
making beadwork at home, so that she could afford to graduate from high school. When Sarah graduated, her hopes for
the future were high: "She saw herself a student in Normal
College, saw herself years later graduating, saw herself a
teacher. Then she would be in another world, toward which
she yearned vaguely but powerfully, and as naturally as a
flower toward light—the world where one had comfort and
could grow. And into this world she would take her parents,
who all their lives had known only hard work and sorrow."[27]
But her hopes were dashed when her father was demoted
from regular wages to piecework, and she had to work full-
time. Gone were her plans to attend Normal School in the fall.
She found a job working for Max Salamovitch, an immigrant
who had saved enough money to quit someone else's tailoring
sweatshop and set up one of his own. It was doing a healthy
business, yet he still pinched every possible penny; working
twelve hours a day, Sarah earned only three dollars a week.
She did not give up her hopes of going to Normal College, and

in the evenings tried to keep up her studies with borrowed textbooks. But after a grinding workday she was often too tired to study, and usually fell asleep over her books.

When Salamovitch discovered that Sarah could read and write English, he had her serve as his translator and secretary, "and soon she was keeping Mr. Salamovitch's accounts and making out his bills. Mr. Salamovitch had said in guarded phrases that he would let her do this 'easy writin' work' that was 'jus' like play' during 'regeler bizniss,' but in practice it developed that business hours were too crowded, and so he had her stay an hour after the girls."[28]

The final episode in Sarah's story came in the aftermath of an accident in the shop. Because Salamovitch delayed turning on the gas lighting until the last moment, a worker named Jenny impaled her finger on a sewing-machine needle in the late-afternoon dusk. Jenny continued going to work, but the swollen finger slowed her down and Salamovitch fired her. Outraged, Sarah quit in solidarity and found work addressing envelopes at three dollars a week and doing beadwork in the evenings. Four days later Sarah received a visit from Salamovitch, who came to offer her her job back. Despite his flattery and entreaties, she refused to go back to the sweatshop. He made one last attempt:

> "Sarah, you come by me to-morrow. I gif you a fine raise, you see." He watched her closely. "I'll let you do only de writin' in my bizniss."
>
> "That's all I do where I work now."
>
> "But I gif you more money. Four dollars a veek!"
>
> Again the impossible thought returned to her, and with such swiftness that she sat dazed by it. She stared into the tailor's round, bearded face, and her eyes grew brighter and brighter.
>
> Mr. Salamovitch spoke again. "Vell, Sarah?"
>
> The great desire to seize this impossible chance that might be possible steadied her. She had a momentary vision of herself mounting the college steps.
>
> "I'll come on one condition," she said, quietly, with firmness. "If

you'll let me do your work after two in the afternoon, and in the evenings."

Her steady gaze, the finality of her voice, took Mr. Salamovitch aback. She was no longer the "leetle girl." He gazed at her with awe, then he thought a moment.

"Vell," he drawled, as he stood up, "so vy not? But, Sarah"—he smiled ingratiatingly—"you von't say not'in' about dis to de odder girls?"[29]

End of story. Sarah's new hours and her raise in pay would now allow her to go to Normal College during the day. In essence, she had become Salamovitch's secretary, and from that position she would presumably go on to become a teacher. In this story, clerical work is clearly seen as a stepping stone for a working-class woman to move up in the class structure, into "the world where one had comfort and could grow."

In *The Long Day: The Story of a New York Working Girl*, Dorothy Richardson also saw clerical work as a means of escaping the drudgery of working-class jobs. Her heroine started out in jobs that were typical of most turn-of-the-century working women: making artificial flowers or paper boxes and working first as a sales clerk and then as a demonstrator of a new brand of tea or coffee in a department store. Determined to better her position, she took a night-school course in stenography and studied English grammar and composition on her own. After having attained a typing speed of one hundred words a minute, she sought her first clerical job. It "paid me only six dollars a week, but it was an excellent training-school, and in it I learned self confidence, perfect accuracy, and rapidity. Although this position paid me two dollars less than what I had been earning brewing tea and coffee and handing it over the counter, and notwithstanding the fact that I knew of places where I could go and earn ten dollars a week, I chose to remain where I was."[30] Armed with clerical experience, she then moved on to a fifteen-dollar-a-week stenographic position at a publishing house. It was at this point in her life that Richardson's heroine started writing and selling articles. Richardson's account shows not only that she considered clerical work to be a cut above other kinds of working-class jobs, but also that she believed that one could use office work as a means of moving from a purely working-class job to a higher position with some autonomy.

The number of women available to work in offices was also augmented by the decline of productive work in the home. For farm families, there was ample work both in the field and in the home to keep the various family members busy. In addition to all of the chores that accompanied farming itself, there was a lot of work that served to keep the family self-sufficient and relatively independent of the market. Even after rural Americans no longer performed such tasks as weaving cloth or making candles, which had been part of the normal household's work in the seventeenth and eighteenth centuries, much still remained. Vegetables and fruits were preserved, butter and cheese were made, some furniture was constructed from scratch, and almost everyone's clothes were handmade. In addition, the absence of running water, central heating, and electricity meant that water had to be carried from a well or pump, wood chopped to supply cooking and heating needs, and kerosene lamps filled and kept in good running order. There was plenty of work to keep parents and children occupied most of the time.[31]

But with the move from country to city that was well under way by the end of the nineteenth century, productive work done in the home began to decrease. The same growth of industrialism that drew a labor force to the cities resulted in the mass production of consumer goods. Items that had been produced in the home were now available in stores. Canned goods, bakery bread, and readymade clothing gained gradual acceptance in more and more urban homes, despite the fact that a kitchen garden plot was a common feature of many urban dwellings into the twentieth century. Even more important changes perhaps, were running water and indoor plumbing, central heating, and electrical wiring, all of which became standard features of more and more urban homes, beginning with those of the well-to-do.

The decrease of productive work in the home had its most dramatic effect on women. "Woman's place is in the home" made economic sense when there was plenty of work to be done. But as domestic work diminished, women who remained there began to lose their productive function in society. In fact, as Gerda Lerner has pointed out, one of the long term developments of the nineteenth century was the elevation of this nonproductive function of women to a symbol of high status and wealth. The "lady" was living testament to her husband's or father's ability to earn money and to a relatively high place in the class structure.[32]

A woman's ability to enjoy nonproductive leisure was determined, of course, by her family's economic position. Booth Tarkington's Alice Adams and her parents were anxious that she should enjoy just as much leisure and luxury as the town's bourgeois daughters. A good example of the way Alice liked to spend her time is this account of her activities on the morning of a high-class dance given by one of the girls in town.

> "Where are you going?" [asked her mother].
> "Oh, I've got lots to do. I thought I'd run out to Mildred's to see what she's going to wear tonight, and then I want to go down and buy a yard of chiffon and some narrow ribbon to make new bows for my slippers—you'll have to give me some money."[33]

Alice would have preferred to spend her time on such frivolous errands, but her family's financial straits sent her into the labor market, her hopes of rising into the bourgeoisie dashed. The relatively small amount of productive work done in the Adams home permitted the grown daughter to spend most of her time in leisure activities, at least for a while. And when Alice entered the labor force, she was able to do so because her labor was not needed in the home.

During the period from 1870 to 1930, the number of occupations open to women was relatively limited. In general, women found employment in factory work of various kinds, in the smaller manufacturing concerns that employed sweated labor, behind the counter in retail stores, in domestic service, in nursing, in clerical work, in teaching, and to a very small degree in some of the higher-level professions. Manufacturing and other factory work, as well as domestic service, did not require literacy. And in positions where neither bills nor orders were written out, neither did retail selling. A literate woman who used her education in her work was restricted to a narrow range of occupational choices. Among these options, the better-paid were clerical work, teaching, and the various professions.[34]

The teaching and professional positions that were open to women absorbed a small proportion of the female labor force. (See Appendix, Table 4.) In fact, teaching was the only occupation requiring literacy that in any way rivaled clerical work as an employer of women after the Civil War. As the data in table 4 illustrate, teaching employed more women than did the clerical occupations until 1900, after which the number of female clerical workers rose so dramatically that teaching fell far behind. Elizabeth Baker argues that women may have preferred clerical work to teaching because of the severe restrictions placed on the personal and social life of teachers. Women teachers were not allowed to smoke, to drink, or, in some instances, to "keep company" with men. Those who married were often asked to leave their jobs. And sometimes "the new view of science and religion which they were bringing to the classroom from their college and university experience was opposed. Conditions such as these prompted many young girls to take up stenography instead of teaching when they graduated from high school; and it is not surprising that more than 100,000—a sixth of the teachers—were reported to have left the profession every year."[35]

There is also some evidence that teachers were paid less than clerical workers. In 1912 the superintendent of schools in Council Bluffs, Iowa, argued that the student who completed the high school's business course was in a better economic position than the one who chose the classical course: "If a graduate of the classical course in the . . . high school had decided to teach in the public schools of the same city, under the most favorable circumstances possible she could not have commenced teaching until one year after graduation. Her salary for the third year after graduation could not have been more than fifty dollars per month for nine months, or $450 per year. The average pupil (female) who graduated from the business department of the high school would have received for the same year an annual salary of slightly over $660. A male graduate of the same year would have received an annual salary of slightly over $840. You may judge for yourself of the economic efficiency from the standpoint of salary."[36]

That women's low level of employment in the professions was due in part to outright discrimination is made clear by a study of women in government service published in 1920. It indicates that the federal government primarily hired women as clerical workers and goes on to demonstrate that the civil service examinations themselves (a prerequisite to government employment) discriminated against women and shunted them into clerical positions. (See Appendix, Table 5.)

Some of the very institutions where literacy skills were taught and polished led directly to clerical work. Both private commercial schools and the commercial track of public high schools trained girls and young women for clerical work. Commercial schools, where skills such as arithmetic, penmanship, and bookkeeping were taught, had been established in the United States by the 1840s and 1850s. Their doors were open to both men and women. Men were urged to obtain an education that would give them a solid start in their climb to success in the business world. Women were encouraged to apply their brains to pursuits other than gracing the domestic circle, or, in the case of working-class women, to aspire to jobs that would liberate them from the drudgery of the factory or sweatshop.

In the latter half of the nineteenth century, such institutions were very successful. By 1890 there were over 80,000 students enrolled in commercial schools (by comparison enrollment in grades nine to twelve of public and private high schools totaled 298,000). Women made up only 4 percent of the 6,460 students enrolled in commercial schools in 1871, but they accounted for 32 percent of the 96,135 enrolled in 1894–95.[37]

By the twentieth century, private business schools were being supplanted by other institutions. University business schools were offering training to aspiring capitalists and managers, while public high schools were initiating commercial education departments to teach clerical skills. By 1915 enrollment in the commercial courses of public high schools outstripped that in private commercial schools.[38] In these high school courses girls predominated. In 1902–3 they already made up 54 percent of the total; in 1930 this had increased to 67 percent.[39] It has been argued that public commercial education furthered the feminization of clerical work. Not only did the commercial courses provide clerical training for girls, but school guidance materials often funneled girls into commercial courses and advised them to plan for clerical jobs.[40]

Several factors, then, conspired to push literate women into clerical work. First, only a few of the occupations where women found employment in significant numbers actually required literacy. While a literate woman would not necessarily seek to put her educational achievements to use in her job, the fact that jobs that demanded literacy were generally better paid would induce her to do so. Second, among the occupations where literacy was needed, only teaching even came close to clerical work in affording employment opportunities to women. This was particularly true after 1900. Third, the lack of job opportunities in the professions was due in part to outright discrimination against women. Finally, some of the literacy training available to girls directed them straight into clerical work.

The demographic characteristics of women clerical workers

differed significantly from those of women workers in general. They tended to live at home more, as opposed to living in boarding or with their employer. Those who lived at home were less likely than other working women to be the sole breadwinner in their household. And women clerical workers were more apt to be single than were women workers as a whole. At the turn of the nineteenth century, the overwhelming majority of female clerical workers were white and born in the United States. For example, in Boston in 1883, 93.6 percent of all female clerical workers were born in the United States.[41] By contrast, only 54.7 percent of Boston women in all occupations were native-born. By 1883 the major immigrant group in Boston was Irish, and Irish women made up 26.8 percent of all Boston working women. Among female clerical workers, however, only 1.4 percent were Irish-born. The situation had not changed significantly by 1900.[42] At that time, 53.1 percent of all female breadwinners in Boston were white and had been born in the United States; 43.6 percent were white foreign-born; and 3.3 percent were black. Among clerical workers, the distribution was considerably different: 85.8 percent were native-born whites, only 13.9 percent were foreign-born whites, and there were literally no black women counted as clerical workers.

Boston was no anomaly. The figures for the United States as a whole show that an unusually large percentage of female clerical workers were native-born.[43] In 1890, 90.8 percent of all clerical workers had been born in the United States, while only 8.8 percent had been born abroad, and a mere 0.4 percent were nonwhite. In 1900 the distribution remained virtually unchanged: 91.3 percent of all female clerical workers were native-born whites, 8.3 percent were foreign-born whites, and still only 0.4 percent were nonwhite. The distribution for women in all occupations, however, is markedly different. Only 56.2 percent of United States working women in 1890 were native-born whites, while 20.3 percent were foreign-

born whites, and 23.5 percent were nonwhite. The mix had
shifted very slightly by 1900, when native-born whites increased to 59.2 percent, and foreign-born whites decreased to
17.2 percent. The proportion of nonwhite women workers remained basically the same at 23.6 percent.

Women clerical workers were more likely to live at home
than were women workers in general. In 1900, 75.8 percent of
all female clerical workers in Boston lived at home, while 24.2
percent were "living with employer or boarding." Among female breadwinners in all occupations, however, the split was
more even: only 55.8 percent of them lived at home, while
44.2 percent lived with an employer or boarded. These clerical
workers were much less likely to be the heads of families than
were other Boston working women. Only 3.2 percent of them
were heads of families, while over three times as many, 10.6
percent, of all female breadwinners in Boston were.[44]

Again, Boston did not differ much from the nation as a
whole. Data from the twenty-seven United States cities studied in the 1900 census show that 81.7 percent of all female
clerical workers lived at home, and only 18.3 percent were "living with employer or boarding." But of female wage earners as
a whole, only 64.8 percent lived at home. Female clerical workers in the twenty-seven cities were also less likely than female
breadwinners in all occupations to be the heads of their families: only 3.3 percent of the clerical workers headed families,
in contrast to 11.9 percent of all working women.[45]

Female clerical workers who lived at home were less likely
to be the only breadwinner in the family than were working
women in general who lived at home. In Boston, only 9.1 percent of female clerical workers were the sole breadwinners in
their family units in 1900, as compared to 16.4 percent of
women working in all occupations.[46] Overall, in the twenty-
seven cities only 8.0 percent of female clerical workers living
at home were the sole wage earner, while 13.9 percent of all
working women living at home were.[47]

Finally, female clerical workers tended more often to be single than did working women. In 1900, 92.8 percent of Boston's female clerical workers were single, compared to only 79.8 percent of Boston working women on the whole. According to the 1900 census, 92.7 percent of all female clerical workers were single, compared to only 76.3 percent of all female breadwinners.[48]

The aggregate data provide the rough outlines of the position of female clerical workers in relation to working women in general in the United States during the late nineteenth and early twentieth centuries. It is fair to say that clerical workers were somewhat better off than other working women. During this era, massive waves of immigration were flooding the United States with vast numbers of foreign-born workers. Many of these could obtain only poorly paid, low-status jobs, and were as mired in the lower strata of the working class as were black women, most of whom ended up as domestic servants. Given this context, it makes sense to assume that any occupational group made up chiefly of native-born whites was in a favorable position.

Other aspects of the demographic profile of female clerical workers support this conclusion. The fact that clerical workers tended to live at home more than other working women does not in itself mean that they were better off. But when this is coupled with the fact that clerical workers who lived at home were less likely to be the only breadwinner than were other working women living at home, it seems clear that clerical workers were somewhat better off economically than the average working woman. Furthermore, the sketchy wage data available show them to have been relatively well paid during the late nineteenth and early twentieth centuries, so that their own contribution to a family unit's income was likely to be quite substantial.

Women clerical workers, whether they came from working-class, small-farm, or small-business families, worked because they had to, and not simply to amuse themselves or to earn a little extra spending money. As Elizabeth Sears, who worked in an office, pointed out in 1917, "what reasonable person will believe that a girl will crowd to work every morning, rain or shine, because she wants extra pin-money that she has no time to spend?"[49] Earlier, she had stated quite matter-of-factly that women worked for economic reasons:

> It would never have struck me to apologize for the fact that I worked for my living. All the girls in my town expected to earn their own living. Most of us went to work as soon as we were graduated from college or high school, or from the condensed form of instruction known as the business college. In that Middle West town no girl dreamed of remaining at home as a burden to the family to support. Sometimes strict necessity urged us forth suddenly from homes that had been a shelter and an inspiration, and sometimes we were only too glad to leave those homes and earn comforts elsewhere. When we met a new girl, we did not ask, "Who is she?" We inquired, "What does she do?"[50]

Sears by no means viewed the need to work as a calamity. She argued instead that economic independence was a definite benefit, and illustrated her point with the tale of a woman who was financially controlled by her father:

> Not long ago a woman was telling me most pathetically that she had been forced to give up her club work. She was a victim of the old regime when every man was the overlord of his own household. She was thirty years old and unmarried, and she said her father had refused to pay her club dues any longer because the members had invited Emma Goldman, in a fit of broad-minded liberality, to speak before the club on an extremely innocent and unexciting subject. She regarded me rather dubiously when I told her I thought it served her right for expecting her father, at her age, to pay her club dues. She still feels that she did right in attending the lecture, for she says it broadened her mind considerably to think that the club had advanced to the point where they would admit Emma Goldman, even though it was mainly out of

curiosity. But she acquiesces meekly in the refusal of her father to continue to pay her club dues. You see, she is a slave to her job of being a daughter and a parasite upon her father's bounty.[51]

For wome women, participation in the labor force afforded psychological benefits such as increased independence and self-reliance. This, however, should not distract attention from the central fact of working-class life: most women worked because they had to.

5

The Ideological Debate

When women first started to work in offices, their presence
was regarded pretty much as an oddity, and either praised as a
courageous experiment or castigated as a ridiculous mistake.
For example, an 1875 engraving showed a shocked man entering an office "taken over by ladies." They were preening themselves before a mirror, fixing each other's hair, reading
Harper's Bazaar, spilling ink on the floor—in short, doing
everything but an honest day's work. The engraving made
women working in an office seem ludicrous.[1] Only in the
1890s was the question of such work for women debated in
earnest. By then female office workers were no longer an oddity, and the sheer weight of their increasing numbers seems
to have provoked a debate that was taken dead seriously by its
participants.

The controversy over whether or not women should engage
in office work took place within the context of the broader debate about whether or not women should work outside the
home at all, a debate that endured throughout the period of
this study, 1870 to 1930. The more specific question of female
office work was still hotly disputed in 1930, forty years after it
first surfaced. That this was so seems surprising. After all,
fully a quarter of all employees in clerical occupations in 1900
were women and by 1930 they made up half of this workforce.
(See Appendix, Table 4.) Furthermore, the percentage of
women was much greater in certain sectors: in 1880 they constituted 40 percent of all stenographers and typists, exceeded

75 percent in 1900, and made up over 95 percent by 1930. (See Appendix, Table 1.) But as long as people were still arguing over whether or not woman's place was exclusively in the home, the question of women as office workers would continue. That it had become moot was irrelevant.

Those opposed to female clerical workers used three arguments: first, that "woman's nature" was not suited to clerical work; second, that women were physically incapable of such work; and third, that women were taking jobs away from men.

"Woman's Nature"

Opponents of female clerical workers maintained that women had been trained to be, and were destined to become, wives and mothers. Domestic concerns, it was argued, were critical to the development of women's character. These had made them the standard-bearers of a higher moral code than existed in the workaday world outside the homes, or, as some claimed, had allowed them to become flighty and temperamental, protected as they had been from the mundane necessities of non-domestic life. No matter how it was defined, femininity was an integral part of women's personalities. And, argued opponents of women office workers, that femininity was inappropriate to clerical work or was in danger of being forfeited to the harsh realities of office life. Women simply would not survive as clerical workers; or if they did, it would be at the expense of their precious femininity. Both interpretations led to the same conclusion: women should devote themselves exclusively to that domestic sphere that was their original destiny. If women were unsuited to the rigors of clerical work, they should stay at home anyway. And if their femininity and consequent ability to be good wives and mothers would be damaged by office work, then it was not worth the sacrifice.

The case for the female office worker rarely challenged this view of woman's nature. In the first place, virtually no one

suggested that woman's domestic role was not her most important one. Instead it was argued that office work actually
made women better wives and mothers: it provided training in
being systematic and well organized, which would be useful
in future household management, and it offered an opportunity to experience first-hand the daily problems that their
future husbands would face. Second, women's higher moral
caliber—on which all agreed—would not be lost in the office.
Rather, it would improve the business world. Third, defenders
of women office workers tended to deny that women were
flighty and temperamental. Finally, they argued that, while
women certainly were possessed of femininity, they were in no
danger of losing it in the office. They also assumed that, once
married, female clerical workers would leave the office, femininity intact, to go off and build their domestic nests. Some
supporters of women office workers thought that it was possible for women to be both wives and office workers, although
no one seemed to think it possible to combine motherhood and
a day at the office. The feminist argument—that women's potential had never been tapped, and that women were entitled
to try any employment—was unusual indeed, even among the
most ardent defenders of female office workers. It suggested,
after all, that domestic life was not necessarily the goal for all
women, an unmentionable and unforgivable violation of the
dominant moral code and of fixed gender-specific roles.

One of the opening shots fired by the opponents of female
employment was Marion Harland's article, "The Incapacity of
Business Women," published in 1889. Harland did not equi-
vocate: "it will be taken for granted that men conduct all
branches of what is known as business—manufacturing, merchandising, professional, and even educational—more systematically and successfully than women." [2] To prove his point,
Harland compared the typical male and female office worker:

> The office-boy is ruled up sharply by line and plummet, not only as
> to work, but deportment. He must be punctual, move quickly and
> quietly, leave all thought of frolic and out-door companionship be-

hind when he crosses the threshold of his place of business; he must be prompt and respectful in speech to employers, and civil to customer, client, and caller—or he goes! The girl stenographer and typewriter "giggles and makes giggle" with the girl book-keeper, and has tiffs (audible) with her enemy, the "old-maid" cashier. One and all, when reproved for negligence, breach of rules, or inefficiency, they retort, or sulk, or—most likely—snivel!

The explanation for this state of affairs lay in "the fact that women look forward to marriage as a definite means of support, and hold but loosely that which they may be called upon at any moment to give up." As a remedy for their incapacities, Harland recommended that women "undertake the allotted labor with the forceful purpose of performing it as if it were the one and only object in life." For, he concluded, "the steadfast industry, the discipline of speech and conduct, the concentration of thought and energy upon the matter set before one for accomplishment, that are essential to business prosperity, are the best conceivable preparation for the high and holy sphere of wife, housekeeper, and mother."

Shortly after Harland's article appeared, another writer, Clara Lanza, also took up the subject of the proper "woman's sphere." But this time the argument came down solidly in favor of female clerical workers, "the work of a clerk being admirably adapted to the sex." Lanza asked the head of a large publishing house whether he preferred to hire women or men as clerical workers:

"Women," was the answer, "are much to be preferred for a number of reasons. They are capable and industrious, and, so far as my personal experience goes, absolutely reliable. Besides, a woman is more conscientious about her work. . . . I wouldn't take men in place of these girls in any circumstances. Men are troublesome. They complain about trifles that a woman wouldn't notice. The office boys don't suit, or the temperature of the building is too hot or too cold, or the light is not properly adjusted. Then, if they have a slight headache, they stay at home. Most of them are married, and their wives fall ill or their mother-in-law comes on a visit, and all these things are made an excuse for absence. The women come whether they have headaches or not. They never want a day off to attend a baseball match. They undertake the work with a full understanding of what is required of them, and they are steadfast in the performance of their duties. We treat them well and never refuse to grant them any trifling favor.

Lanza also claimed that businessmen preferred female stenographers because they were better trusted with business secrets. While admitting that some hired women because their labor was cheaper, she maintained that "efficient women can command as high salaries as men." Lanza found that "the girls make good wives."

There is nothing in clerical training that detracts from the finest womanly qualities, and men have outgrown their admiration for feminine helplessness and have come to look upon independence as something worth having. Clerical training educates the mind to accuracy in details, punctuality in the daily affairs of life, economy in the adjustment of time and quickness of perception. Perhaps this is the reason why so many men choose a wife amid the deft-fingered clerks in preference to the society misses. The woman clerk has studied the value of concentration, learned the lesson that incites to work when a burden bears heavily upon her strength. She knows the worth of self-reliance, and the fine courage that springs from the consciousness that a good result has been accomplished by a well-directed effort.[3]

There are several interesting aspects of Lanza's argument. The critique of male clerical employees can be found elsewhere, and virtually word for word, in criticisms of female office workers. Moreover, her support for women in offices was based on "woman's nature," the rationale for Harland's opposition. But since Lanza concluded by noting that many clerical workers eventually married and what good preparation clerical work was for matrimonial life, she left the impression that women's ultimate goal was just what Harland had affirmed: the "high and holy sphere of wife, housekeeper, and mother." Harland and Lanza were at odds on the issue of women office workers, but their assumptions about woman's nature were identical.

One of the qualities ascribed to nineteenth-century women, or at least to those from bourgeois or professional backgrounds, was a high level of moral idealism. Their finer moral spirit, it was argued, would be damaged if they entered the dog-eat-dog world of the business office. Theodora Wadsworth Baker in *Harper's Weekly* weighed the benefits and losses that would occur if women's idealism and business pragmatism were mixed. "Experience in business," the author concluded, "broadens a woman's mind and makes her views more practical." While "it may rob her of some of her romance, . . . the experience which is a substitute for it is far more valuable. She will be less of a dreamer, and more of a thinker."[4]

Moral idealism and moral superiority were, for Baker, part of "woman's nature." Such beliefs apparently took a beating after 1910. So did the argument that women should not work in business offices because their fine-spun spiritual ideals might be sullied. Notions about woman's nature partly shifted after the 1880s and 1890s, and so did the grounds used in arguing that her nature made woman unsuitable for office work. By the 1920s woman was no longer portrayed as the protectress of higher values. Instead, she was depicted as scatterbrained, unable to concentrate on the business at hand in the office, too temperamental and emotional for the impersonal world of work.

In 1920 an article entitled "The Feminine Failure in Business" depicted the potential female office worker as a well-to-do woman speculating about what she would do if widowed. She would start a business career "modestly enough, private secretary to the president of a big bank or corporation or something of that sort." But her eyes would be fixed on matrimony, and the corporate president would be unable to resist the "pathetic and lonely" sight of his secretary dressed "simply in black and white—half mourning, you know."[5] Another writer cautioned against using women as reception clerks: "It is just as inadvisable to have a girl at the reception desk. Nine out of ten girls are temperamental. On one day they are likely to flirt with every male vistor. On another day they are likely to be flippant. On still another they are likely to be unduly sarcastic. The tenth girl, who possesses the right qualifications for the reception desk, can be utilized in a more responsible position."[6] The theme of woman's unstable temperament was still being sounded in 1929. An article on "The Temperamental Typist" claimed that certain women regarded "their inability to get along with their fellows as a special gift from Nature." Such pride in moodiness prompted many employers to complain and wonder why their female employees could not "forget their own personalities for a few hours a day."[7]

Significantly, critics of women office workers no longer urged women to leave clerical jobs; instead they merely complained about their behavior. Clearly, the number of female clerical workers had grown so large that even their opponents had to accept their presence. Some even admitted that a few women were able to overcome the handicaps inherent in woman's nature. But those who did so were then accused of losing their feminine qualities and becoming "mannish." Counseling against this danger, one writer concluded that women office workers would have been better off had they never left the home. Contact with the business world tended to make woman cynical, severe, and falsely independent. Gone would be her "pretty superstitions, her treasured beliefs in men, and her happy, careless, girlish little ways." Fascinated by the excitement of business, the "very young woman" would forego the prospect of "tame housekeeping": "her immature judgment is not capable of giving correct values to the things of life."[8]

Others argued that it was entirely possible for a woman to maintain her femininity in the office. Harriet Brunkhurst cited the case of a woman who carefully distinguished between her positions as worker and woman in the office where she worked alongside her husband: "I take my share of the office work as a man partner would, no favors and no shirking. It is business, not pretense with us. At the same time, if I forget my umbrella, I would not think of returning for it, nor would I think of going upstairs for something he could get for me. I am his wife, not his business partner, then."[9] One of the few to recognize that there were drawbacks in a life exclusively devoted to home and family, Brunkhurst argued that a married woman could be of great help to her husband in his business. Her activity, moreover, would keep the mother of grown children from having too much time on her hands and meddling unhealthily in their lives. Even the woman whom she quoted, who required chivalric deference from her husband, did not look forward to returning to the isolation of her home.

The claim that office work did not rob women of their femininity was generally invoked. Rather than defining "femininity" in different terms, supporters of women clerical workers were, by and large, content to turn opposing statements on their heads. Some, however, depicted women in terms markedly different from the conventional perspective, suggesting that women were perfectly capable of clear, efficient, rational intelligence: to oppose women entering the office because of some mistaken notion about their "nature" was ridiculous. George Gissing's *The Odd Women* is in large part the story of two English women, one of whom, Mary Barfoot, inherited some money and set up a school to give salable skills, particularly stenography and typewriting, to women who had to work.[10] The second woman, Rhoda Nunn, was paid a salary to help Barfoot with the school. Both women were feminists intent on endowing women with skills and values that would enable them to make their way in the world on an equal footing with men and would provide them with concrete economic alternatives to marriage. Gissing describes Mary Barfoot as a woman who "could have managed a large and complicated business, could have filled a place on a board of directors, have taken an active part in municipal government—nay, perchance in national."[11]

Barfoot challenged those who argued that women should leave office work because they were displacing men. She did not contend otherwise. Rather she defended women office workers on the ground that women were entitled to develop their potential: "If woman is no longer to be womanish, but a human being of powers and responsibilities, she must become militant, defiant. She must push her claims to the extremity. . . . I don't care whether we crowd out the men or not. I don't care *what* results, if only women are made strong and self-reliant and nobly independent! . . . There must be a new type of woman, active in every sphere of life; a new worker out in the world, a new ruler in the home. Of the old virtues we can retain many, but we have to add to them those which have been thought appropriate only in men." [12]

Gissing was one of a select company who did not assume that women's ultimate goal was a domestic life of housekeeping and motherhood. The heroine of "His Wife's Place," for example, had dual motives: economic necessity and the desire to build a good life for herself and her husband. Nonetheless, her idea of a woman's capacities, and of her appropriate role, differed sharply from that endorsed by opponents of women clerical workers. "His Wife's Place" described the dispute that Carter and Mary Payan, a young married couple, had after the husband's return from overseas military duty during World War I. Mary, in his absence, had returned to her premarital work as office manager for an automobile dealer. By the time Carter returned, she was earning four thousand dollars a year. She had bought many of the home furnishings they had planned to save for, and had also managed to put two thousand dollars in a savings account. Carter returned to his old office, but earned annually seventeen hundred dollars less than Mary. Stung by his own image of the proper roles for husband and wife, and needled by acquaintances because Mary commanded such a high salary, Carter demanded that she quit her job and return to the home. She refused: "To her way of thinking, four thousand dollars a year was four thousand dollars a year. It had a concrete meaning to her of investments which should return them an income so long as they lived. . . . She wanted that. This was not because she was essentially mercenary, but she was eminently sensible. Investments and an income meant safety; it meant a family solidity which nothing else could give."[13]

Angered by Mary's response, Carter again demanded that she quit. She again refused and, after a bitter argument, he walked out of the apartment, about to leave town for good and give up on their marriage. But she urged him to seize a business opportunity as manager of a car agency. He would have to borrow from a bank, and live off his wife's earnings until the agency was established. Mary tried to persuade him:

> "Don't you see the wonderful chance, if only you will look at it in the right way? We have pooled our lives, Carter. Why not, for just a little while, pool our earnings so that—oh, so that we can have a real family?"[14]

Carter was tempted, but manly pride made him reluctant. However, he changed his mind upon seeing the bank president, who complimented him on having a wife as practical and talented as Mary and also told him that the condition for a $10,000 loan would be her guarantee:

> "Do you know," said the president, "that a wife like yours is the greatest asset a man can have? I thank God my wife was like her. We married on nothing. I was a grocer's clerk. She was a dressmaker. We made a partnership of it for the first few years; both of our backs were to the wheel. We saved enough so, at twenty-five, I could start a tiny grocery in a country town. She helped. Every cent she made we saved—and when the store was started she kept the books, and on Saturdays worked behind the counter. Those were different days—in those days marriage was a real partnership, and both parties gave it all they had. It seems to be different now."
>
> Carter stared at the president. He had seen his wife, a handsome, wonderfully gowned woman apparently a *grande dame*. She

was a leader in society, a woman universally admired for her character and for her ability and for her culture. It did not seem possible.

"She made me," said the president. "It wasn't her savings alone,
but the force she put behind me. She compelled me to succeed. It
looks to me as if your wife were the same sort."

"Times have changed," Carter said weakly. "I am twitted about
it."

"By imbeciles," said the president sharply.[15]

Women's Physical Capacities

Although the main argument against female clerical workers
was that woman's nature and office work did not mix, and that
woman's place was in the home, other objections were also advanced. Women, for example, were considered physically or
biologically unsuited to such work. An article of 1920 on "The
Feminine Failure in Business" blamed woman's physical in-
feriority on her menstrual cycle:

> In the case of girls past their adolescent period there are physical
> obstacles to success in business which every employer of women
> in offices and shops fully understands. The loss of the services of
> women employees for several days each month is a serious prob-
> lem where salaries are paid regularly and the "docking" system for
> absences is not in practice. The fact that women are less strong,
> less agile, less enduring under continued mental strain than men,
> makes it evident that woman in contest with man must be granted
> something more than a fair field and unrestricted competition.[16]

A male stenographer for the U.S. Congress, who recorded con-
gressional pontifications, offered his opinion on why women
were not employed in this occupation: "they haven't the physical endurance. A reporter has to have the constitution of a
Missouri mule."[17] In 1929, the author of "The Temperamental
Typist" felt that the physical reasons given for women not
working in offices had been repeated so often that there was
no need for him to do so.[18]

The debate over whether women or men were physically more fit for office work had been going on for quite some time. Even *Scientific American* had examined the question "Are Men Better Typists than Women?" in 1913. It sought an answer in some "interesting scientific tests" done by a certain J. M. Lahy. What emerged was an unintentionally hilarious account of tests measuring muscular sensibility with the "myo-esthesimeter," the strength of the hand with the "Regnier-Cheron dynamometer," the tactile sense with the "Weber compass," and auditory reaction time with the "d'Arsonval chronoscope." After detailed descriptions of these various instruments, with careful attention paid to their degree of accuracy, the results of testing six women and five men, judged to be "strictly comparable" (exactly how they were comparable was not explained), were summarized. "Good women typists," Lahy found, demonstrated "tactile and muscular sensibility," an "excellent memory for letters," and "keen and sustained" attention; but they had a "relative slowness of auditory reaction." For their part, the men "surpass women in rapidity of auditory actions and, consequently, in speed of work, but are inferior to women, perhaps, in power of sustained attention." Lahy ended by acknowledging that his sample was too small to be conclusive and that his results "are merely indications which may be confirmed or invalidated by future researches."[19]

These "indications" provoked a response from C. E. Smith, the author of *Practical Course in Touch Typewriting*, who favored women office workers, arguing that women surpassed men in manual dexterity. He also claimed that a typewriter keyboard was more suited to women than to men, since the latter were often handicapped by their "extremely large and strong fingers." This was "especially the case when all the fingers of the hands are employed in striking the keys, which is the only scientific method of operating a typewriter."[20] Having made the case for women's greater manual dexterity, Smith went on to observe that many women had won typewriting speed contests and concluded that "the fact that nearly all of the world's work in this line of endeavor is in the hands of women, and that in open competition for so many years they have carried off the premier honors, seems to me to be worthy of consideration and to entitle women to be considered equal, if not superior, to the opposite sex as typists."[21]

That women did not have the physical endurance to withstand the grueling pace of office work was the biological grounds for opposition to women clerical workers. Their menstrual cycles, presumed to incapacitate them several days out of every month, were also cited. Proponents, however, usually asserted women's greater manual dexterity when calling upon biology to support their position. This emphasis on female manual dexterity was a double-edged sword. For it could justify the contention that woman's place was indeed at the typewriter, but not much higher in the office bureaucracy.

Displacing Men

The third issue that repeatedly cropped up in the office-work debate was that of women displacing male workers. Opponents of female office workers argued that women prevented men from getting good wages. Such deprivation in turn reduced the number of men who were financially able to marry and support their wives. Eleanor Whiting, for instance, affirmed that "sometimes [men's] wages are cut because of the competition of women; sometimes they are displaced altogether by women. The young man who should marry and become the head of a family finds himself displaced at the counter or in the office by a young woman who may be obliged to struggle single-handed with poverty for years because the man who is her social mate cannot afford to marry her."[22]

In 1909 a "successful business woman" wrote a cautionary piece, "Why I Will Not Let My Daughter Go Into Business." The author had been married to a man incapable of sustained, diligent work who moved from job to job, always dissatisfied with something or other about his position. Finally, fed up with what she regarded as her husband's shiftlessness, she took on the work that he had just quit and made a success of it. Meanwhile he stayed home and took care of the house and children. One summer night, when her husband and children were away on a vacation that she could not afford the time to take, the "successful business woman"

> suddenly realized that John was not working at all, or at least just at intervals, earning enough so that he did not ask me to give him carfare or spending money. . . . Lying in the dark that night there came to me the sickening truth; I was supporting a man—a healthy, able-bodied, clear-brained man. . . .
>
> In the gray light of dawn I sent a telegram to my father. He came and said it was quite true. The world agreed with him and with me that I was doing my sons, my fine, straight-limbed lads, a grievous wrong in showing them the example of a father who "lives off" his wife's—a woman's—earnings. How did I expect to make men of them with such a man sitting at the head of the table?
>
> And again I chose the easier way. I secured a divorce![23]

But she now had to work hard to regain her children's affection, lost through the years of neglect. In the denouement, she learns that her husband had not only remarried, but had at last become a "successful man."

> Some said that the shock of divorce and separation fom his children had steadied him. Others said he had married money and had taken a fresh start. But I *knew*. He had married a woman who had done that in which I had failed—made a man of him. . . .
>
> If I had grappled with my husband's weakness as I had with the problem of self-support!
>
> It is too easy today for the woman to get into business. It is too easy, I say, for the family life, the domestic purity, the moral standard of our nation.[24]

The message was obvious: for reasons of family stability and emotional health, rather than finance, women should not displace men if they had any choice in the matter. The "successful business woman" directed her advice explicitly at the "woman who does not have to become a wage-earner"[25] and had only pity for those women forced to work for financial reasons.

George Gissing's *The Odd Women* contained the most direct response to the complaint that women were displacing men in office work. Male clerks, Mary Barfoot stated, "doubtless had a grievance. But, in the miserable disorder of our social state, one grievance had to be weighed against another, and . . . there was much more to be urged on behalf of women who invaded what had been exclusively the men's sphere, than on behalf of the men who began to complain of this invasion."[26]

Harriet Brunkhurst, who was a staunch defender of women office workers, also countered the male-displacement argument. In most cases, she pointed out, the woman's wage was very badly needed. Drawing upon the case of a girl named Cecil, she noted that the mothers of working daughters who expected them to share fully in the housework had failed to recognize changes in their daughters' status.

> That their support is absolutely dependent upon Cecil's remaining "fit" the mother knows; but that recreation is necessary to maintain the condition she cannot grasp. Consequently, when Cecil takes Sunday morning for the little fussy tasks about her wardrobe the mother sees only sheer perversity, to say nothing of incipient depravity, about it. And there is the incontrovertible fact that Cecil "has all her evenings free." Moreover the mother wails: "She never has time to do anything for me!" It does not occur to her that she is asking of Cecil, whose strength already is fully taxed, more than she would ask from a man. She is the type of woman who would say of her husband: "John is so tired when he returns from work!" That Cecil may be tired she never considers.[27]

In 1917 Brunkhurst advised working women to forego domestic tasks lest they become overworked and nervous. Implicit in this advice was the assumption that women working in offices did so out of necessity, and that for them to try to fulfill the function of housewife as well was foolhardy. That they displaced men in offices may have been true, but financial need, not choice (as the "successful business woman" had argued), drove them. Instead of looking on them with pity, as that successful woman had done, Brunkhurst was more interested in lessening their burdens.

The Function of the Ideological Debate

Though many clerical jobs had been feminized by 1930, discord over the change continued. As noted earlier, it was only part of a larger and long-enduring debate on the whole subject of whether women should work outside the home at all. This partially explains why critics were still bothering to attack or justify women working in offices long after their employment was well established. The debate had another function, one that its participants were at best only dimly aware of: many of the assertions and conclusions of both sides served as ideological confirmation for the sexual stratification of the office labor force and for the concentration of women in lower-level work.

With the exception of Gissing's heroines and of Harriet Brunkhurst, participants in the debate assumed that woman's ultimate goal was to become a wife and mother.[28] Supporters and opponents of female office workers differed only on whether office work assisted or damaged women in their preparations for matrimony and maternity. The conviction that woman's place was in the home served to justify her restriction to lower-level clerical work. If women eventually were going to stop working to marry and have children, what was the point of promoting them to managerial or even higher-level clerical positions? To do so would be a waste of resources and training. Furthermore, women whose hearts were set on future family life probably did not care that much about their work in the office. Or so the argument went, and thus did it legitimate their segregation in the lower-paid, lower-status jobs.[29]

The manual-dexterity argument was used repeatedly as

evidence that women made better typists than men. Since they did, small wonder that such a high percentage of typists were women. The concentration of women in typing jobs was thereby neatly justified.

A comparison of management policies concerning messenger boys and girls provides an interesting example of the way in which the ideological assumptions about men and women buttressed their respective positions and futures in the office. Although their policies were formally stated at about the same time, these companies seem to have been at different stages in the development of a highly stratified office workforce with rigid promotional channels. In 1923 one group of companies still regarded the position of messenger as an excellent springboard to managerial positions, but clearly the reference was to messenger *boys* only: "The Scott Company reports in one of its bulletins the results of a survey made in three nationally known companies of the messenger-boy situation. 'Messenger and office boys are of particular interest because they are so definitely a source of supply for future executive material. Messenger work offers a splendid chance to learn in an intimate way the methods and policies of a company. This is an educational opportunity that should be made available only to those who are capable of taking advantage of it.'"[30] The policy of the Hupp Motor Company, stated two years later by its office manager, was altogether different: "The first radical change [in the messenger department] was the substitution of girls for boys. . . . It was immediately found that girls were more amenable to discipline. . . . A few months serve to tell whether a girl has special adaptability for any line of higher work we have to offer. Some are given the opportunity to practice typewriting during the noon hour. These girls usually take courses in typing at night school. Others seem better fitted for clerical work. Promotions to minor positions in other departments are made in accordance with the capacity of the particular girl."[31] No more talk of "future executive material." A messenger *girl* at the Hupp Motor Company could hope to aspire only to a "minor position," and she was more likely to end up behind a typewriter.

The point here is that different assumptions were made about sex-linked characteristics. When the position of messenger was a training ground for executive positions, boys were characterized as "a natural and logical source of supply for higher positions." But when promotion led at most to a "minor position," boys were said to have a "natural tendency to boyishness and play" and to be less "amenable to discipline" than were girls. Thus the ideological assumptions about the natural characteristics of males and females were made to mesh very neatly with the way in which clerical work was organized. Assumptions about women helped to justify not only a situation in which women were clustered in the lower levels of a work organization, but also the very fact that such positions, devoid of much chance of substantial promotion, existed at all.

6

Scientific Management
in the Office

By the beginning of the twentieth century, offices had grown so large that some employers were becoming concerned over their inefficiency and lack of discipline. The amount of paperwork had mushroomed rapidly in many offices, and, in the eyes of some employers, the clerical workforce had become unwieldy. Consequently, schemes for reorganizing office work to eliminate inefficiency and extract a "fair day's work" from the staff began to be promoted. Such plans were soon being called the "scientific management of the office," which is not surprising in light of the popularity of Frederick Winslow Taylor's principles among industrialists. And indeed the features of scientific management in the office had much in common with the scientific management of the factory.

In general, scientific management was the effort to develop "scientific" methods of measuring and managing work. To that end, tasks were analyzed and broken down into their component parts, after which "experiments" were conducted to determine how each could best be completed in the shortest possible time. Having determined the "one best way" to do a job, scientific managers then set out to impose these "scientifically proven" methods upon workers. For all the scientific terminology in which the new managers couched their ideas, it is well to remember that these ideas first developed within the context of capitalist production. Such being the case, it is helpful to think of their efforts as an attempt to arrive at the one most profitable way to organize labor. After all, scientific managers were not intent on controlling workers and the labor process for the mere sake of control; they sought control for the sake of higher profits.

The scientific management of the office hinged on developing quantitative measures for various tasks. Much like their industrial counterparts, office managers conducted time and motion studies on typists, stenographers, and other clericals with a view toward determining the optimal workpace. Armed with such "objective" measurements, scientific managers could then proceed to the next steps in reshaping the office. They could develop standards that would determine how long it should take to do various office tasks, and also break down these tasks into their component parts. This provided a detailed map of office work and the basis for organizing the office itself. They considered it essential to dictate the details of the entire work process, not just for workers but for managers as well. For in redesigning the office, they did not confine themselves to instructing typists how to type and file clerks how to file; they also told managers how to manage.

Another aspect of scientific office management was more directly concerned with maximizing profitability. This entailed assigning office tasks to the lowest-paid workers possible and trying to fit the right worker to the right job. According to this principle, the more highly paid stenographer should never do work that could just as easily be done by a lower-paid typist. It assumed that one could find clerical workers who were "naturally" suited to this or that niche, and that they would remain in it for the length of their job tenure.

Scientific managers paid close attention to the physical arrangement of the office. Their plans for rearranging the layout and purchasing equipment were guided by two objectives: to

make the paperwork flow as efficiently as possible, and to encourage workers to concentrate on their tasks. Even when
they discussed such physical improvements as better ventilation or lighting, they were more concerned with increasing
output than with the intrinsic value of a healthy working
environment. Finally, having reorganized office work, some
scientific managers still found themselves faced with the
problem of motivating clerical workers. Although they mainly
handled this by setting standards and penalizing delinquents,
they also used techniques for jacking up office morale.

The effort at making the office more efficient—so that as
much work would be completed in as little time and for as low
a cost as possible—led to changes that diverted control over
the work process from clerical workers to managers. Workers
and managers rarely referred to it in those terms, but control
of the work process was very much at issue. It had been central to the changes in the organization of clerical work from
the time when, to a certain extent, it resembled a craft, to the
time when it had been degraded to a series of routinized, repetitive tasks.[1] In the movement to apply the principles of scientific management to the office can be seen the crystalliza-
tion of this change in the organization of clerical work.

The Need to Reorganize Office Production

In 1913 the Remington Typewriter Company published an
eight-page advertisement that began with this story:

> The President of a large manufacturing business had just re-
> turned from his semi-annual tour of the various plants of the con-
> cern located in other cities.
> He felt in a very good humor with himself and the world in gen-
> eral, because his visit had shown very clearly that certain effi-
> ciency ideas which he had suggested on his previous visits had

been successfully carried out. In one plant the output had been increased over 125 percent, at the same time that an actual reduction of about one percent in operating expenses had been effected.

Naturally, he was inclined to pride himself a bit upon his efficiency achievement.

As he passed through the outer offices on the way to his own, he was struck by the noise and confusion that seemed to prevail. It was 10 o'clock in the morning, yet salesmen were lounging about, gossiping with each other. One stenographer sat doing nothing, while the executive she was attending sat on the corner of the desk talking to a visitor from the outside. One stenographer was cleaning her machine, another was peeling an orange and joking with the office boy. Some of those who were working would puzzle over their notes a little while, then turn to their machines with a burst of activity, then stop and repeat the process.

Altogether, to the President, fresh from his efficiency triumphs, there seemed to be a most astonishing amount of lost motion, wasted energy and mismanagement somewhere—right in his own office. . . .

This instance typifies an anomalous situation in the business world.

Efficiency principles have been applied to industry, commerce, and even to other branches of office work, but not, as a rule, to the management of stenographic service.[2]

Since the company was primarily interested in selling typewriters, the ad concluded by pushing Remington machines as the key to stenographic efficiency. The manner in which Remington chose to approach prospective customers reflected a concern with "inefficiency" in the office that was quite widespread after 1900. This preoccupation with inefficiency was caused by two developments in office work: an extensive and rapid growth in the volume of office work to the point where the older methods of organizing office production simply could not keep up with the increased workload, and the inability of many employers to discipline clerical workers effectively. These problems were, of course, connected. If the amount of paperwork had not grown so large, a lack of discipline on the part of clerical workers might not have seemed so serious. For the purposes of analysis, however, it is useful to separate them. The response of most businessmen to these problems was either to hire more clerical workers or to replace those who were "lazy" or "insubordinate." But there were also some employers, at first few in number, who responded by restructuring the office itself. By the second decade of the twentieth century, their efforts came to be referred to as the scientific management of the office.

The following gives a sense of the problems confronted by the manager of an office where older methods of office production prevailed.[3]

There are about 20,000 names on the mailing list, which was arranged in two massive volumes. The classification was alphabetically by surnames. Only the name and post office address were given. There was no provision to record the advertisement from which the name was secured; whether the bearer of the name ever sent in an order; or, in the case of such an order, how much the order amounted to. Thus it was impossible to keep weeding out the "dead" names. . . . The only signal for striking out "dead" names was that postmasters would sometimes take the trouble to report their inability to deliver the catalogue. . . .

The correspondence of the firm was filed in old-fashioned pocket letter files, dividing the alphabet into about twenty parts. There were about thirty of these files filled almost to bursting with retail mail orders, wholesale and jobbing orders, and all sorts of letters, including the manager's personal letters, freight way bills, requests for the catalogue, and the like. Whenever there was a complaint from a customer, the manager very properly insisted on seeing the original order. During the busy season of about four months, two or three clerks were kept busy a large part of their time in hunting out letters and orders from the mass of papers. The correspondence amounted to about 60,000 pieces a year, and each year's letters were kept together. Thus, with twenty divisions of the alphabet, there would be an average of 3,000 papers in each division, and to find a letter it was possible that the entire 3,000 papers would have to be handled.

The author attributed this chaos to the fact that the firm's manager was ignorant of "modern business methods" and reluctant to give up on traditional ways of doing things. "When it was suggested to [him] . . . that the mailing list should be card indexed, he replied that he had never heard of a card index, or card catalogue; and it turned out that he was unfamiliar with vertical letter files and all other modern devices."[4] But the total breakdown of the old system during a Christmas rush persuaded him that some changes were warranted, and he agreed to install a card index system for the mailing list and a new method of filing correspondence. The former made it possible to record the dates and amounts of up to twenty orders for each customer, as well as the location of the advertisement that had brought in their business. "One of the valuable features of the cards is that they show who the good customers are, and these customers can be given extra good treatment." The new vertical letter files separated out wholesale and jobber correspondence from that of retail customers, which was placed in folders that divided the alphabet into two hundred parts. "This reduced the average number of papers in each division to 200 instead of 3,000; but as the plan was to transfer the correspondence to storage files every six months, the average would be less than one hundred letters."[5]

The advantages of this reorganization were manifold. There were monetary savings: the card-index system was said to save $2,000 a year and the vertical letter file another $1,000 in labor no longer spent in hunting up letters. Other advantages cited were "increased efficiency in many ways, a very great reduction in friction [presumably between clerks and their bosses], and the lessening of liability to errors in filling orders."[6]

As the volume of office work multiplied, forcing employers to devise new methods of organizing production, so too did the problems entailed in disciplining clerical labor. Disciplining clerical workers involved more than ensuring that they came to work on time or were at their desks for the requisite number of hours each day, although that was part of it. It also covered such matters as specifying exactly how numerous tasks were to be carried out and keeping employees sufficiently motivated so that they would neither sabotage their work (unwittingly or otherwise) nor quit after a relatively short time.

The issue of who controlled the execution of tasks was often joined most sharply in offices where clerks had been employed in the same position for many years. A bookkeeper who had held his job for years, for example, would be loath to give up his own particular procedure for keeping accounts, even in the face of a rapidly expanding workload. An article published in 1906, "The New Science of Business: Making An Office Efficient," described this conservatism:

> We have had the same shipping clerk for more than twenty years. He is familiar with all of our customers, indeed, I think he knows most of them personally, and he used to carry their shipping directions in his head. Every now and then he would route his goods wrong, and there would be a dispute. No records were ever kept of shipping directions given by customers, but his memory which was excellent, was always relied upon in case of trouble. But we cannot afford to have continual disputes with our customers, even over trivial matters, and *after a great deal of very hard work* I got him to use a vertical file for shipping directions as they were sent in, so that we should be able to refer to the exact letter in which shipping directions were sent to us. . . .
>
> *I found the deepest conservatism among the bookkeepers. The men who handled the ledgers were the hardest ones to deal with that I ever saw.* A loose leaf ledger was the first thing I began with. It took me three years really to get the loose leaf ledger system well established in our cashier's department. I didn't want to offend the cashier, because he had been with us a long time, and he had handled from seven to ten millions of money every year and we had never lost a penny—but he was quite certain that there were great dangers connected with the loose leaf ledgers which we should never be able to overcome. In fact, he thought that without the old-fashioned hard-backed ledger he really would not be safe— he was afraid somebody would run off with the leaves. And besides, it was a modern thing, and didn't appeal to him. However,

we got it in. We have four of them now, and even he would not part with them for a great deal.[7]

In both instances, the clerk was reluctant to relinquish methods that had been used for years and that, especially in the case of the shipping clerk, had afforded him a fair amount of autonomy. While the efficiency expert bemoaned the clerks' conservatism, much as industrial engineers complained of "shop culture," the control of the work process was clearly at stake. Such examples from 1906 hint that wresting control from the hands of clerks was not always easy, and there are indications that this struggle persisted. In 1922 another author complained that "most offices are still run in the 'good old way.'" He also indicated that getting employees to cooperate with reorganization was not always an easy matter: "As a preliminary to eliminating this inadequate and obsolescent scheme of management, and placing office work on a controlled and planned basis, it is first necessary to make an analysis of what is actually being done. This information must, of necessity, come from the clerks themselves, and may be obtained by requiring them, for a period of one month, to make a daily memorandum report of what they did and how long it took to do each task. *This requirement, it goes without saying, must be put into effect with a great deal of tact.*"[8] The last point comes as no surprise, considering that the clerical workers were being asked to submit to much closer supervision.

Many businessmen had trouble getting their clerks to work all of the minutes they were being paid for. William Henry Leffingwell, who was to the scientific management of the office what Frederick Winslow Taylor was to the scientific management of the factory, told how one company went about dealing with this problem.

First, an effort was made to get everybody in the office to put in a full day in the office. There is a manifest tonic in punctuality. But this organization, which as I have already indicated, was at least up to average standards, taking it by and large, not only started late, but stopped early. The employees were getting ready to quit from 15 to 30 minutes before closing time, and there were other losses almost as great around the noon hour. So instead of the nominal 7½-hour day, there was in effect something like a 6½-hour day.

The management first of all handled this situation with this notice to employees:

"1. The hours will be changed from 9 a.m. to 5 p.m., and every employee will be expected to be on time.

"2. At the telephone desk on the ground floor will be placed a time sheet which each employee is to sign upon arriving, the first employee to arrive to sign on the first line, the second on the second line, and so on. At 9:00 a.m. an employee delegated by the office manager will draw a blue line below the last name written up to that time. At 9:15 a red line will be drawn under the last name at that time. The period between 9:00 and 9:15 will be considered the period of grace. Those names appearing below the red line will be considered late. Those whose names appear in the 'period of grace' (between 9:00 and 9:15) twice in one week will be considered as being late both times.

"3. At 9:30 this sheet is to be taken in by the office manager. Any employee who fails to sign the time sheet will be considered as absent and subject (in the discretion of the office manager) to have the time deducted from pay. If an employee arrives after 9:30, he or she is to sign a special sheet to be obtained from the office manager.

"4. Once a month the names of those having a perfect record for the month will be posted in all departments. Those whose names appear on this bulletin will be considered the employees who are cooperating with the company.

"This applies to all employees."[9]

While Leffingwell boasted that such an inspirational missive eliminated tardiness, the fact that employees ran the risk of having their paychecks docked was probably just as important as pure exhortation. The disciplinary problems typified by this example were hardly subtle: clerical workers shaved minutes here and there, and their employers were just as determined to stop them. In this case, as in many others, the clerical "soldiering" brought a very simple punishment—you don't come to work on time, we don't pay you as much. Period.

A related problem was described by the director of the Independent Efficiency Service in an article of 1916 on office efficiency: "By alternating the positions of slow and fast workers, a total net gain is reached, as the rapid clerks by spirit and example hasten the sluggards. Two girls who naturally gossip and chew gum should not be located alongside each other—granted that they belong in a business at all."[10] The problem here was how to keep clericals at work while they sat at their desks; the remedy was manipulation rather than outright punishment. Instead of having a supervisor constantly oversee the staff, the article recommended that managers manipulate their workers into silence by structural means.

A third problem was the absence of "employee motivation." While many employers traced workers' slothfulness to laziness or insubordination, some attributed it to low morale. Just such an assessment was made about the fifty employees in the bookkeeping department of one large firm:

> It was found that most of the girls were dissatisfied. . . . A short talk with one of the best girls brought out the reason for this, and it seemed ridiculously simple on the face of it. Leaving out the head of the department and her assistants, the rest of the girls were just a large group of just so many bookkeepers. There was little or no chance for an individual to distinguish herself. If her work was well done, she did only what was expected of her. But if she happened to slip up just once, she soon heard of it, from both customers and department heads.[11]

The manager recommended reorganizing the department along the lines of "the Army system of management." He was quite pleased with the results of separating the "girls" into six squads, which were set up to compete against each other. Not only did the bookkeepers now each belong to a "distinctive group," but they also had the chance to win a paid half-day off if their group finished its work by the deadline. Furthermore, the proliferation of ranks within bookkeeping—there were now a "captain," two "lieutenants," six "sergeants" and six "corporals"—had increased opportunities for promotion. The manager claimed that this reorganization, together with pay and vacation incentives, increased morale and forged a dutiful labor force.

Extent of Scientific Management

It would be difficult to determine precisely how many offices had been reorganized along principles of scientific management at any particular time. Nonetheless, two points about the extent of the scientific management of the office may be made. First, many firms remained relatively untouched by scientific management by 1930. Most of these firms were relatively small, but there were also many larger businesses that simply continued to increase the number of clerical workers rather than reorganize the ones they already employed along more efficient lines. Second, although scientific management did not affect all firms, it represented a concerted and self-conscious drive by a vanguard among businessmen. It did not consist simply of the sum total of various unrelated schemes to reorganize office production. Rather, it was pushed forward in part by a group of capitalists and managers who saw their role explicitly as spreading the gospel of scientific management in order to make capitalism in the United States more efficient and profitable.

Some firms remained unaffected by scientific management because employers often blamed low productivity or even financial failure on individual incompetence rather than on poor organization. The very fact that proponents of scientific management in the office were so evangelical indicates that many capitalists and managers were either ignorant or skeptical of their methods. Recent analysts of work relations within the office have also been skeptical. They argue that scientific management as practiced on the factory floor was in general not appropriate to the office. The majority of English offices, David Lockwood argues, had not, by 1958, been greatly affected by the rationalizing trend in office management; people have been fooled into thinking otherwise because "the most advanced developments in the field are likely to divert attention from the normal division of labour." Only the very largest offices, he claims, which in England accounted for merely a small proportion of all clerical workers, could afford to invest in machinery, such as the "Hollerith machine," that lent itself to scientifically managed work organization.[12]

Lockwood's warning not to overestimate the impact of scientific management on the office is well taken, since it would be silly to ignore the fact that many offices, particularly small ones, even now remain quite traditional. On the other hand, there is good reason to believe that he overstates the case, particularly if one extrapolates his view to offices outside of England. There is evidence, for the United States at least, that offices did not really have to be all that large for techniques of scientific management to be introduced.[13] A manager convinced of the superiority of a scientifically managed office would not need to wait while his office staff of fifty grew to five hundred before reorganizing office production. As the literature promoting scientific management shows, an office manager bitten by the bug of scientific management was just as prepared to "rationalize" the work of one or two clerical workers. Furthermore, scientific management did not apply exclusively to those clerical workers using office machines. Quantitative measurements and production standards could be prescribed for a wide variety of office chores. A file clerk, for example, who worked solely by hand, might be expected to meet certain production standards, whether these involved filing a sheaf of letters or retrieving documents from the filing cabinets.

Lockwood's work commands our attention because it represents the received wisdom about the nature of office work. His arguments—that the small size of the office and the very nature of the tasks performed in clerical work made it impossible for employers to devise quantified, routinized criteria—are ones often cited to deny the popularity of scientific management in the office. But the literature on the topic indicates otherwise. It was not only scientific managers themselves who concluded that the "rationalized" office was the wave of the future. In 1929, at the meetings of the American Academy of Political and Social Science, Grace L. Coyle stated that "in many offices today, scientific management is being applied to all the clerical functions. . . . The actual extent of such scientific office management is no doubt proportionately small, but it is significant in that it is in the van of those movements which are likely eventually to affect the entire clerical field." [14]

Coyle was certainly right: a movement had begun to bring about the scientific management of the office. Its foremost proponent was William Henry Leffingwell, who churned out numerous articles and two long-winded studies, *Scientific Office Management* (1918) and *Office Management: Principles and Practice* (1925). A self-proclaimed missionary in the crusade to bring enlightened office management methods to a benighted business community, Leffingwell wrote in the preface to *Office Management*:

> a pressing need exists for a thorough understanding on the part of business men in general, and office managers in particular, of the fundamental principles underlying the work of that pioneer of scientific management, the late Frederick Winslow Taylor. . . .
>
> I have attempted in this work to explain the scientific basis of office procedure, and at the same time accord to the profession of office management the dignity and position it deserves. I am not aware that any writer has previously attempted this task. [15]

Leffingwell assumed the mantle of proselytizer because he was persuaded that few people understood the importance of the office manager's job. He was convinced that office management was the wave of the future, if businessmen would only realize that a scientifically managed office would bolster profits.

> There is . . . a brilliant future for those office managers who have arrived at the recognition of the office as a major function of business and the equal importance of the work of office management with every other business activity. When these men set themselves to discover the range of possibilities of scientific office management, and make it their profession, they will substantially advance the interests of their company, effect large savings, and thereby greatly add to the profits of the business, while at the same time forcing the more or less reluctant admission of the vital importance of their work from other executives.[16]

Leffingwell was only one of many writers who pressed for adopting Taylorism in the office. Their writings were published in two magazines: *Industrial Management*, which promoted scientific management in both factory and office, and *System: The Magazine of Business*, "a monthly magazine devoted to the improvement of business method." Founded in 1900 as a compendium of short articles explaining a wide variety of office techniques, *System* seems to have enjoyed a fair amount of success, since it soon became larger and fancier. For thirty years it published articles about all aspects of business management, but concentrated on managing the office workforce at both the executive and clerical levels. In September 1929 it became a weekly, and changed to its current name, *Business Week*.

The existence of such publications, as well as Leffingwell's studies, indicates that scientific management had a growing readership in business circles. Capitalists and managers in increasing numbers took it for granted that the scientific management of the office was desirable. Indeed the concerted efforts of Leffingwell and his colleagues had an influence on the business community that was disproportionate to their numbers.

The Characteristics of Scientific Management

Despite the relative coherence of the movement towards scientific office management, there was no clear pattern to office
reorganization. Office managers and "efficiency experts" usually tailored their schemes to the requirements of the individual office. The wealth of literature on the subject mainly consists of a series of detailed descriptions about the changes
made in one particular office or a list of helpful hints about the
minutest details of office procedure.

Several larger areas of concern emerge out of this welter of
detail. A primary problem was to determine exactly how long it
took to complete specific tasks. Some employers boggled at the
prospect of making such calculations. Leffingwell described
the typical dilemma of an office manager: "The nature of the
work, being so varied, did not make for great speed, and it was
a simple matter for a clerk to show all appearances of being
diligently performing her work, when as a matter of fact she
was not accomplishing half the work she should. No amount
of watching would have discovered this. As a matter of fact,
with two girls who were working side by side, we found that
one did fifty percent more than the other. The slow one said: 'I
have all of the "stickers."' Before we set standards, we had no
means of disproving her statements."[17]

Such soldiering on the part of clerical workers led management to conclude that the quantitative measurement of office
work was the necessary first step in the drive to get more work
out of its employees. In 1913 a method for measuring stenographic output was described in *System*:

> By beginning with the machine [the typewriter] and making a
> continuous record of its operation, it will be possible to learn how
> much time is lost, the causes, and what can be done to remove
> them. As often as not, the causes of inefficiency will be found to be
> conditions over which the stenographer has no control—particu-
> larly if her work is the taking of dictation from a department head
> with "many irons in the fire."

Such a record of the work of a typewriter for one full day of eight hours is shown at the head of this article [The record consists of a circular paper graph, marked off by the hour and minute, on which the times during which the typewriter was in use are recorded by an ink line.] The forenoon record is for correspondence only. The stenographer who did the work ranks high at dictation and machine operation and for a long time has been the personal stenographer for the head of a department in a large manufacturing concern, hence was perfectly familiar with the work. At the noon hour all the work given her had been completed.

Her full time ran from 8 a.m. to 12 m., four hours. The record shows that nothing was done on the machine except to open and put it in order (see short line at 8:34) until 9:15, when one envelope was addressed and two others at 9:25. Real work on the machine was not started until 9:54, her time until then being taken up in opening and sorting mail, and taking dictation.

From 9:54 the machine was kept going steadily until 10:59, one hour and four minutes. Then there was a stop of forty-two minutes (three envelopes being addressed in the meanwhile) for more dictation. The work was resumed for fifteen minutes, until 11:57, when the machine was closed for noon.

The only possible way to prevent the recorder from tracing an accurate history of the day's operations is to close the contact at the machine, thereby causing the pen to make a continuous heavy line on the chart. Its smooth edges and even width make it quite different from the broken and wavy heavy line made by the typewriter when the operator is working fast and hard.[18]

This description raises some interesting points. The subjects of quantitative study were usually the more efficient or loyal employees. Thus office managers often did not rely on abstract notions to set the work rate. Instead they based their estimates on the output of clerical workers from whom they thought they were getting "a fair day's work." Moreover, office managers assured themselves of trustworthy results by using recording devices that could not be rigged.

Managers were especially concerned about wasted motion. As one of them, campaigning to streamline the work of his typists, put it, "the preliminary survey revealed also that the girls were doing work foreign to their principal operation of typing. These operations interfered with the operators' speed; and they could easily be done by somebody else. The next step was to relieve the girls of these details—on the same general principle by which a hodcarrier relieves a group of bricklayers from the fetch-and-carry part of their work."[19]

Having identified his problem—an insufficient division of labor—this manager then set out to solve it. First he had an office boy assemble the sheets of typing and carbon paper. He figured that each typist had been losing up to a minute per letter in collating the sheets and the carbons. Although it was still the typist's job to separate the carbon paper from the completed typewritten sheets, the manager tried to eliminate any "waste motion" in this task by using carbon sheets larger than the sheets of paper. "The operator grasps the sheaf of copies with her finger and thumb at the trimmed corner, grasps with her left hand the projecting lower edges of the carbon sheets and pulls all the carbon sheets out with one motion. The little time-saving counts; but the bigger, really worthwhile saving comes through not breaking the girl's typing pace."[20] Finally, he reduced the time typists had been "wasting" in fetching their own dictation cylinders (there were no tape recorders in 1920) by having the supervisor deliver them. This also relieved a typist of the chance to "choose the [cylinder] she considered most easy."[21] After completing this reorganization of the division of labor, the manager smugly surveyed the benefits:

> Having combed the work of unessentials and reduced the job entirely to typing, unhindered by details foreign to it, we were ready to spend the second week in finding out what each individual girl could do under these conditions. So we had a measuring and recording device attached on each machine. As the speedometer on your car ticks off the miles, so the speedometers on the girls' machines tick off their accomplishment. The difference between the reading on any girl's machine at the opening hour and at noon gives the number of points of work she did that morning. There is

nothing indefinite about her record now, no way to mistake the truth about the good or bad work.[22]

Despite the fact that some office managers got quite carried away with measuring the work of their clericals, so that the measurement sometimes became an end in itself, the drive to quantify clerical work was only a first step. Once an office manager had developed and taken the quantitative measurements, he proceeded to the second stage of setting work standards and then figuring out methods to enforce them.

Since office procedures varied greatly, writers were hesitant about prescribing a specific standard. Instead, they tended to concentrate on the principles and general method of setting standards, as did this author in 1917:

> The next step is the determination of the standard. There are dozens of conceptions of what a standard is. At one end are those maintaining that the standard should be the unattainable ideal of absolute perfection, while at the other end are those who maintain that standard should be a point to be reached by honest and ordinary effort. To my mind, standard is that point in production representing the highest figure which can be reached, and which with conscientious and true effort can be maintained. It makes no great difference what method is selected, but pick the one best meeting your needs and ideas and stick to it. Standard is, of course, the 100 percent figure of efficiency; your workers may exceed this figure or not. Theoretically no one should ever be able to exceed 100 percent, but practically it makes no difference and there is a psychological something in making it possible for the high average worker to reach this figure which outweighs the inconsistency of having a very few exceed it.
>
> Determine next, therefore, what plan the standard will be classified under, then by a study of past records, by intimate knowledge of the work, by time study, and by any other means in your power determine this figure. Check it and counter check it—take no chances—spend all the time necessary at this point; a wrong standard is a dangerous thing. If too low, you will be unable to make an attractive offer to the worker, and this might necessitate raising the standard which is a disastrous proceeding.

On the contrary, if the standard is too high, workers will make little money and will become discouraged.[23]

The author was very careful to set standards that would not need to be changed in the future. This concern, it seems plausible, resulted from the difficulty of getting clerical workers to accept or adjust to new standards.

For enforcing standards, office managers resorted to variations on one basic strategy. This amounted to rewarding clerical workers monetarily if they attained the standard, and docking them monetarily if they did not. The office manager of a rubber company, for instance, described his method:

It is assumed that each clerk will equal or better the standard on every task assigned to her. At the beginning of each week the supervisor credits her with the maximum bonus, which is $3 for the week. Each time she fails to equal or better the standard on a job the supervisor debits her one point, meaning that 10 cents will be subtracted from her $3 bonus.[24]

Sometimes employers found it necessary to pressure employees to meet the standard. A favorite tactic was to foster competitiveness—as among stenographers in a Chicago office: "Every morning the number of lines each has written the day before is posted on the bulletin board to foster the spirit of friendly rivalry in the department."[25]

Forcing clerical workers to meet management-dictated standards was an essential step in the scientific management of the office, and one that some employers had difficulty in making. For instance, the managers in Leffingwell's office had set a standard of 200 square inches per hour for each typist, and promised to reward those who met it with a bonus of ten cents for every hour that they held to it. (Weekly wages varied from $7 to $15). None of the typists thought it possible to attain this level, since they had been averaging 127 square inches per hour. Even after the managers conducted "rest and fatigue" studies and decided to institute two twenty-minute breaks every day when "all employees [were] encouraged to go outside and play . . . the girls all insisted that the standard was too high."

> At about this time one of the girls who had been below the average in speed was offered a prize of one dollar for the first hour she reached the standard. The very next day she came down to work determined to win that dollar. After several hours spent in the attempt, she won the prize. That broke the ice. It *was* possible, after all. The same prize was offered to all the girls in the department and thereafter, day after day, one after another won it until finally reaching the standard became a habit.[26]

By inducing one of his slowest workers to meet the standard, Leffingwell employed one of the basic tactics of scientific management. Those familiar with Taylor's work will no doubt recognize it, since he used the stratagem in manipulating the famous worker, Schmidt.[27]

The managers also addressed the work process itself. This included every sort of detail from organizing the filing system, to arranging office furniture, to "efficiently" employing the labor of a skilled stenographer. Office managers sometimes directed their attention to the most minute detail in dictating exactly how clerical workers should execute their tasks.

> After several days of patient teaching, a young man persisted in making a large number of useless motions. I walked up to him unexpectedly, grasped his hand and held it for the time usually occupied by his useless motions. Then I pointed out the result. I had not interfered with his work.
>
> He grasped the point and one or two days thereafter reached the standard. So well had he learned that the best work is accomplished by a minimum of motions that he studied his job intently and soon with very little effort earned the maximum bonus given for 120 percent effectiveness. Formerly he had become tired out trying to perform 50 percent of the task set.[28]

Leffingwell did not always interfere so directly, and generally contented himself with simply telling clerical workers how to do their work. He urged typists to operate their machines "slowly and deliberately" rather than in erratic spurts, in order to eliminate time lost in erasing mistakes; instructed them in the "one right way" to insert pieces of paper into the typewriter; explained the correct method for sitting at their desks, which was "to sit well back in the chairs, with the feet placed squarely on the floor and head and shoulders erect"; and encouraged them to remember twenty-five words or so from a manuscript each time they looked at it, so they would not get a crick in their necks from constantly turning their heads back and forth.[29] Other "experts" had their own pet directives. George A. Ricker, for example, had "two fixed requirements for our stenographers: first, they must use pens instead of pencils, for a pencil is a poor substitute for the ever-sharp pen point; second, they must operate the typewriter by the touch system, for this adds much to their speed."[30]

What is striking about these directives is their specificity. They indicate that precious little was left to the clerical workers' discretion. Here is Leffingwell, for instance, on how to attach sheets of paper to each other:

> The pinning or clipping of papers is another problem that comes up in nearly every office. Few clerks, it seems, know how to pin papers so that everything but the top sheet can be read without unpinning. Often the sheets are pinned two or three inches from the top. The next person who must read the papers has to un-pin and re-pin them.
>
> It is simple, with a bit of study, to see that the pinning is done right in the first place. Different classes of papers, of course, may have to be pinned differently. Some require the envelope on top, some on the bottom, some demand a particular sequence, and so on. The problem is worth careful study, for the thousands of papers handled in the average office have to be pinned on an average of five or six times, if there is no general rule of pinning right in the first place. This means a loss of possibly from .05 to .10 of a minute for each pinning. If 1,000 sets of papers are handled in a day, and pinned and re-pinned half a dozen times, this amounts to from three hundred to six hundred minutes a day—a total loss.[31]

Leffingwell seems to have been at one extreme in this drive to control the clerical work process. Not all advocates of scientific office management dwelled on the finest details of the work process. Somewhat more subtle were the managers at the Curtis Publishing Company who "found the workers continually adding small details, often unnecessary, in their routine. [These] girls . . . would fight hard to retain their individual pet ideas." Management was content to let the "girls" keep their "pet ideas," confident that their bonus system would lead them to reject "inefficient" methods and to implement only those that increased production or had managerial approval.[32] Homer Pace, acting deputy commissioner of the Internal Revenue Service, faced with the problem of reorganizing his 1,000-person staff to process tax returns more efficiently, did not—unlike Leffingwell—concentrate on the details of the work process. Rather, he encouraged his division heads to reorganize themselves and, pleased with the results, he stated: "The new methods are substantially what I should have chosen. But there is a tremendous weight of public opinion behind them that would not be there if they were my work alone. Exactly the same plan might easily have been a flat failure if I had promulgated it by myself."[33] It should be emphasized that such autonomy in reorganization was granted only to the division heads, and not extended to the lowliest office worker. Furthermore, the incentive offered to middle-level managers for innovation was not simply a pat on the head, for, as Pace explained, "When I convinced myself of the value of most of our division and section heads, and began to talk to them about the chances of getting more work done, I began talking at the same time about getting them more pay."[34]

The vast majority of scientific office managers were determined to exert increasing control over the work process. Their efforts were often cloaked in terms such as "eliminating waste motion," "increasing productivity," and "improving efficiency." Such terms were invariably invoked in the struggle over reassigning tasks to the lowest-paid worker possible. Put differently, this involved fitting the worker to the job. As one manager said, "In an office of over 100 employees I would never recommend having the mailing and filing handled by the same person. . . . While both require accuracy, mailing requires special despatch and filing special neatness. These two qualities can seldom be found in the same person."[35] Some writers assumed that it was natural to fit the worker to the job; others pointed out that it was profitable. In an article directed to business executives, Floyd Parsons stated that "great waste results from doing little things that can be done just as well by lower-priced employees. Successful executives never write a letter, sharpen a pencil, carry on a telephone conversation, or see a caller, if anyone else in the office whose time is worth less can do it just as well for them."[36] Leffingwell echoed this view. In "What 'Scientific Management' Did for My Office," he described the "memory clerk," who relieved the office executive of the tiresome chore of having to remember appointments, meetings, and other details. Anyone who needed reminding of something in the future left a note to that effect with the memory clerk, who maintained a central file and alerted the executives to their tasks and appointments at the appropriate time.[37]

The interests of scientific managers encompassed labor-saving machinery, and a fair amount of management literature contained advice on how to use this or that device in the most profitable way. Floyd Parsons argued that "in this day of modern labor-saving appliances, it is unnecessary as well as unwise to permit employees to put nervous energy and brain effort into tasks that could be done better, cheaper, and more speedily by dictating, duplicating, billing and computing machines. Such devices pay for themselves in a remarkably short period of time. Mechanical devices are more accurate than humans, and never get tired."[38]

Another aspect of office modernization was the establishment of a proper sexual division of labor. Gender-specific jobs were taken for granted. As a matter of course, executives were referred to as "he" and clerks and stenographers as "she." But on occasion a writer addressed the question directly. For instance, a 1922 article on cost-cutting, by a director of the National Association of Office Managers, advised that "jobs should be classified and those that should properly be filled by male workers segregated from those that should be filled by female workers."[39] Although the author did not elaborate, it seems clear that he considered a sensibly organized office to be one in which men and women were in their proper places.

The well-run office, in which all the workers were suited to their jobs, had to find employees with the right "attributes." At the Curtis Publishing Company in 1913, "the problem was to pick out workers who were temperamentally fitted for the duties of the department and who had adequate training, and to establish a standard day's work and a bonus system of payment."[40] At Curtis, things were organized to such an extent that there was an entire department—the "Employment and Instruction Department"—devoted to the selection and training of employees, and it was to this department that others turned for recruitment. They sent their specifications for a new worker and it then selected the candidate from its file of applicants. This new employee was sent to the "Instruction Division Training School," where she was trained and observed. "Frequently, the girls who have passed the preliminary test and have entered the school are rejected as unsuited either by training or temperament to the work required."[41]

Curtis's procedures prefigured the objective tests for prospective clerical workers that were in full swing by 1920. Its proponents had no use for those who questioned their counsel. As two enthusiasts affirmed: "The evidence is clearly against the old methods of selection by chance, by hiring and firing, by personal opinion, by individual 'hunches,' by unstandardized examinations. There is no going backward for the employer and his employment manager who prefer the old ways. They will be eliminated."[42]

The tests administered by scientific office managers fell

into two general categories: general intelligence tests, and tests of specific clerical skills. There was considerable debate over which was better. One writer did not "believe that office work has any special abilities that have so far been demonstrated," and preferred the general intelligence test.[43] Another argued, however, that "it is usually true that clerks with more intelligence, broader information, good social personalities, and quicker reactions will be able to demonstrate better clerical ability than their less developed fellow-workers. But it is wasteful to attempt to measure clerical ability through such indirect channels as general information, or by mental gymnastics, when it can be measured directly with specific clerical tests."[44] The experts seemed agreed that the best way to judge the efficacy of a test was to administer it to the clerical workers already employed in an office. For example, the Charles Williams Company tested its clericals to see if the results "correlated well with the actual work accomplished. If so, the tests would be useful in selecting future typists."[45] Although it was admitted that the usefulness of these tests had not dawned on all businessmen,[46] scientific office managers were confident that more and more would see the light. They based their confidence on what they considered to be the inherent scientific rationality of fitting workers to their jobs, as well as on a conviction that this part of scientific office management could only serve to improve the Human Condition. After all, it sought to find out

> *what line of activities each one most enjoys*, and so far as possible assigning him to that line.
> Suppose a girl secures an office position involving faculties which in her case have not been developed. She probably does not make a success of the work, nor does she enjoy it, and if opportunity offers she probably solves the problem by resigning while the management is still hoping for some less drastic solution. Such experiences, too common to every office, increase the office turnover, involve economic losses in fruitless training of transients, and discourage applicants.[47]

Advocates of scientific management assumed that each person was endowed with certain "natural" capabilities that automatically suited him or her to a certain type of work. The ideal office workforce would be one in which the "natural" differences between the employees determined their clerical niches. Given this assumption, it is not surprising that they advised keeping certain workers in particular positions. Even when discussing promotions, they meant moving workers into their appropriate slots. They saw substantial promotions as a way of getting office workers to their "natural" level rather than as rewards that every employee could normally expect for conscientious effort.

Testing and placement was part of the process whereby clericals were stripped of control over their work. Since it was assumed that an employee was "naturally" suited to his or her job and only to that job, it was unlikely that he or she would be given the opportunity to learn much about other positions or be permitted the chance to work at them. The consequent segregation of each worker into a narrow scope of activity deprived him or her of the opportunity to grasp the wider operations of the firm or how the employee's job fit in. As was pointed out earlier, this amounted to a diminution of the control clericals exercised over their work.

Just as businessmen and office managers were advised to make the most efficient and profitable use of their employees' labor, they were also counseled on how to use their office space and furniture efficiently. Leffingwell advised office managers to make a map of their office layout and then to "draw lines showing the passage of the work from desk to desk. . . . Nothing will show you so clearly the wasted steps which your employees may be taking."[48] Discussion of physical arrangements usually centered on two objectives: placement so that the paperwork travelled efficiently from desk to desk and so that clerical workers would not be distracted in their work. The desks of one office were all arranged facing away from the door, which "brought about a marked increase in the output of work. Where formerly the employees faced the door or to one side and for the most part looked up from their work whenever anyone entered, they are no longer disturbed."[49] Distractions, after all, made for inefficiency.

Office managers were not concerned only about efficiency. They also cared about control. Writing in 1923, Floyd W. Parsons advised that "if possible, desks should be placed that the workers will be back to back. Cliques destroy team-work and waste time gossiping. Clannish workers should be separated and placed in different parts of the office or in different departments."[50] And in an account of how distractions were cut down in a stenographic department, the merchandise manager of the Greenfield Tap and Die Corporation claimed that the elimination of distractions made it easier to keep stenographers fixed on their chores. Their desks faced the door and the supervisor's desk, so that the comings and goings "broke into [their] concentration. So we turned the operators around, with the girls' backs toward the supervisor. Now a visitor never comes under the view of the operators. The supervisor transmits all orders, choosing her time so as not to break in upon a girl who has struck her pace. Little distracts the operators."[51] Homer S. Pace put the point even more bluntly. According to him, the managers responsible for reorganizing the office "decided that the desks should all be set facing one way, with the supervisor in the rear. *That at once permitted more effective supervision* and made close attention to work easier."[52] It might also be pointed out that this arrangement ensured that a clerical worker would never know when he or she was being watched, and would therefore be more inclined to diligence. The issue of control even arose in the choice of office furniture. One industrial engineer thought that the flat-top desk was preferable to the more old-fashioned roll top, for "the worker is at all times visible to his superior."[53]

Most of the literature on the physical arrangement of the office focused on designing a "rational" work flow and eliminating distractions. But every so often there was a suggestion for office design that on the face of it seemed to have the simple purpose of making a more pleasant place to work. For example, one writer in 1906 described the lunch room that had been part of his office for six years, where the clerical workers ate at the company's expense. But the manager did not only have the convenience of his employees in mind when he praised this facility. "We have easily halved the noon absence of our organization," he boasted. "Better yet, the women instead of going out and drinking a little tea, are sent back to work with something substantial in their stomachs. The men, instead of going to a free-lunch counter, and coming back with the smell of beer on them, have clear heads and we think we can do very nearly as good work in the afternoon as in the morning."[54] At a collection agency in New York City, pains were taken to make the office "artistic" with flowers on a stenographer's desk and pictures on the wall. These interior decorations were justified by the increased productivity they allegedly elicited from employees, who were said to produce 25 percent more than the average stenographer and to be "more amenable to discipline" under the influence of "pleasant surroundings."[55]

Good ventilation and lighting, one might think, would be provided for the simple purpose of keeping clerical workers healthy. But, as an industrial engineer from General Electric indicated, scientific managers were as concerned about productivity as health: "Whether ventilation is for the purposes of giving comfort or of getting additional production, it is mighty important."[56] In another case, an office manager delayed improvements in lighting until worker output was tested under better lighting conditions.[57]

Scientific managers were also worried about getting their clericals to do their work well. As we have seen, profit was the incentive to foster motivation. Leffingwell, for example, suggested that "the worker be encouraged and coached. . . . An employee must never be scolded for not reaching the standard, nor accused of 'stalling.' Once let her get the idea that she is being driven, and the chance for really effective work is destroyed. Almost always, I have found, more can be done by coaxing than by driving." [58] One Michigan office manager, also seeking to encourage his workers, catalogued eight methods for "gingering up office work." Some of his techniques, such as regular exercise periods and an "open window drill" to keep fresh air in the office, were intended to combat fatigue. He also proposed an "efficiency register," which evaluated each worker with ratings based on "application, mental ability, productivity, personality and health" as a means of fostering "a spirit of friendly rivalry." [59] Such methods for maintaining clerical productivity were not unusual. But he also had some less orthodox suggestions. "Workers—especially girls—respond to the inspiration of mottoes," he found, and posted short "mottoes for the week" on a blackboard in full view of the staff. " 'Never Late' cut down tardiness eighteen per cent in a week. 'Be Friendly' had the effect of breaking up an office feud that had perplexed the manager and hindered office routine for many weeks." [60] He also recommended putting flowers on each worker's desk and playing music periodically, in hopes of improving performance. "Sometimes, when a sudden rush of work has tensed the entire organization and errors due to high speed are becoming apparent, a soothing violin solo, or an old fashioned melody, will relieve the tension." [61] Finally, he offered two suggestions for the discussion of office matters. One was a forum: "A general council is held every Monday morning. All workers gather in a large assembly room. Questions are asked and answered. Every one is given an opportunity for frank expression. Knots of tangled routine are straightened and a more sincere cooperation is instituted." [62] There was also a weekly social club—the "All Pull Together Club"—that sometimes featured outside speakers who addressed such issues as morale and the office routine. [63]

That there were meetings at which clerical workers discussed their jobs contradicted the advice of most office management. Scientific managers generally frowned upon such gatherings and thought even less of soliciting workers' opinions. The Michigan office meetings, however, seemed to have served largely as safety valves that had no effect on the way in which office work was organized. But the very fact that they took place at all, and were supported by an office manager, indicates that management could not always depend solely on bonus plans and premium payments to keep productivity high —that non-monetary forms of encouragement might also be useful. By and large, however, flowers, mottoes, and meetings were the exception, material incentives the rule.

The Significance of Scientific Management

The movement to reorganize office work, so central to scientific management, had begun even before scientific office management became a coherent movement during the first two decades of the twentieth century.[64] And, judging from the missionary enthusiasm that still characterized articles promoting scientific management in the late 1920s, there remained converts aplenty to be won over. Office modernization, then, did not commence abruptly with the scientific office management movement. Nor did the full flowering of that movement put those changes into universal effect. Nonetheless, modernization trends may be seen with particular clarity in the drive to apply principles of scientific management in the office.

One of these trends was the elaboration of the division of labor in office work, which owed its particular form to the fact that it unfolded under capitalism.[65] Scientific management crystallized the specialization of labor within the office. Scientific managers studied and measured the component tasks which constituted any particular clerical job. Breaking down office jobs into their component parts, they endeavored to make "efficient" use of the workforce, which involved employing the cheapest possible labor. In the case of the manager who claimed he had "saved 42% on routine work," for example, the division of labor prompted him to have a lower-paid office boy do the job of assembling sheets of typewriter and carbon paper in order that the more highly-paid typist would not waste valuable time on such a mundane task.[66] As far as managers in capitalist firms were concerned, "efficient" was synonymous with "inexpensive."

This division of labor in office work was enmeshed with a second major trend—the diminution of control by clericals over their work. For many office employees, the minute division of labor meant that the scope of their work was reduced to the repeated performance of limited tasks. The clerk in the mail-order house who spent all day opening envelopes and arranging the orders alphabetically; the office boy who did nothing but assemble sets of blank typewriter and carbon paper; the typist who typed letters from dictaphone cylinders from one week to the next, were not in a position to do more than a small fraction of the work that went on daily in a large office. Because their activities were so restricted in scope, they did not have the opportunity to grasp other office procedures or to see how their particular task fit into the work flow. Thus deprived, they could not determine whether their particular tasks had been organized in the most practical way. Denied through their ignorance the possibility of changing the design or scope of their work, they were forced to work as their superiors prescribed.

Furthermore, scientific managers advised controlling clerical work in very direct and explicit ways. From a Leffingwell who grabbed a young man's hand to prevent him from "making a large number of useless motions," to a Charles M. Ripley who arranged his workers' desks so as to prevent their being distracted by passersby, scientific managers were intent on dictating the details of clerical work and removing control over that work process from the hands of clerical workers.

However, the scientific management of the office was not directed at all the people who worked in an office. Scientific managers tended to aim their plans for reorganization at lower-level clerical workers: office boys, shipping clerks, file clerks, typists, and stenographers. The responsibilities of one major category of office worker remained relatively untouched by modernization dicta. That office worker was the private secretary.

7

The Private Secretary

In 1934 the author of *The Personal Secretary* contended that there was a fundamental difference between a stenographer and a secretary. A stenographer needed only the intelligence to understand what was being dictated to her and what she was supposed to do with it, the accuracy to carry out "the routine of her work," the judgment to decide "familiar, easily learned, routine matters," and the loyalty to be trusted with "confidential matters . . . within the relatively unimportant range of routine dictation." Furthermore, "her personality makes less difference, as she comes into contact with relatively few people, practically all of whom are fellow-workers. She seldom meets the outside people on whose good will and opinion the success of the business rests."[1] The secretary, by contrast, was all that the stenographer was not, and performed a much more demanding job.[2]

That a secretary used to be privy to secret matters, and that to this day a "secretary" may be someone in an exalted position, suggests that a clerical worker who was a secretary was quite different from those clerical workers who were stenographers, typists, file clerks, or office machine operators. The latter performed one small segment of a finely broken-down division of labor in a routinized fashion. The private secretary, by contrast, was encouraged to take the initiative in performing tasks and was often entrusted with a very broad range of office jobs.

The Private Secretary's Work

By 1910 attempts to define the difference between secretaries and other clerical workers, notably stenographers, had begun. In 1916 one author described the work of a typist as "purely mechanical." But "the stenographer's work," he argued, "comes a little higher because the stenographer executes the thoughts of someone else. A secretary must think independently, and at the same time execute the thoughts of another."[3] And in 1924, a Carnegie Institute of Technology survey, which included questionnaires distributed to both employers and secretaries, sought to determine precisely what were the duties and traits of a secretary. Employers, the survey concluded, "were all agreed that the stenographer does purely routine work—'she is a diligent, faithful, human machine.'" Secretaries, on the other hand, were said to be distinguished by their initiative, responsibleness, interest in work, and executive ability.[4]

There seemed to be general agreement among employers, secretaries, and those studying the latter that real differences existed between a secretary and a stenographer. The exercise, or lack, of initiative was a major distinction. But initiative was not necessarily inherent; it could be developed. Indeed, stenographers were advised that the best way to advance to the position of secretary was to show some inventiveness. Stenographers who became private secretaries were those who "took upon themselves without instruction from their employers such tasks as the management of callers, the keeping of appointments, and the accomplishment of other detail work of their employers. Because they were wide awake and took an interest in the work of their employers, these stenographers soon picked up many bits of information concerning their employers' business, their methods and policies, and their activities. . . . The more information of this nature they secured, the better able they became to decide upon matters that came up when the chiefs were busy or were away."[5]

People were seldom precise about the meaning of "taking

the initiative," since secretaries would do so in a variety of ways. The general idea, however, was that they should figure out for themselves what jobs needed to be done and how to do them, rather than waiting for work to be assigned. Here, for instance, is how one secretary acted on her own:

> The weeks went on and I had been doing this secretarial work for about eight months, when Mr. Blank was hastily called away on a business trip lasting a fortnight. . . .
>
> He left with a hurried good-by and practically no instructions save that any mail might be held until his return, or, in the event of its being urgent, should be referred to one of his assistants. That wasn't particularly pleasing to me, for I thought that if I were a real secretary I ought to be able to handle that correspondence myself. Then I began to wonder if I couldn't, and then I decided that I would. . . .
>
> In regard to the business material I asked advice occasionally, but on the whole I managed it myself. Visitors I likewise disposed of—graciously, I hope; with celerity, I know. The result was that when Mr. Blank returned there were but three or four matters which actually required his personal attention. I showed him the rest of the material, together with carbons of my replies, and explained how the various affairs stood.
>
> "Why," he exclaimed with a pleasant smile, "it's very nice of you to have kept things up for me in this way! No one ever did it before."
>
> And the next week brought me a ten-dollar salary increase and the practical certainty that I was making good.[6]

Another writer encouraged secretaries to trust their own judgment when it came to introducing new office methods, and cautioned them against self-deprecating thinking such as "It has never occurred to those higher up to adopt this plan. It is only I, a mere hireling, thinking this. I am not paid to think. I am paid to do the things thought out for me by others. Therefore, the thoughts that occur to me are of no value." Instead, secretaries were advised to trust their own experience: "the people who are going to devise the better means of perfecting office work are those whose daily tasks put them in close touch with the faults of the systems now in use." [7]

Employer correspondence was one area where secretaries could assume responsibility. Gladys Torson advised that the secretary capable of "polishing off the boss's letters" should go a step further and "write many of his letters for him. . . . Write as many letters as your boss will let you, because this is one of the ways in which you can be of the most help to the average man." [8] Earlier, another writer had warned that "the secretary should not be timid about undertaking the answering of any letter which is not of such importance in nature as those taken in to the chief." [9] The fledgling secretary, he acknowledged, would at first have to check with his "chief" to assure that the work was being done correctly, but after a while he would be on his own. The secretary can thus be very valuable. After all, "the true executive has not much time for anything but creative work. He can very easily waste two or three hours a day by personal attention to his mail." [10] But there were also warnings against secretaries being too independent: "Too much independence or initiative or individuality—too much 'I' really—almost no employer wishes." [11]

Correcting an employer's mistakes was often left to secretaries. "Theoretically, the secretary is supposed to put down on paper just what is said and just as the dictator said it. As a matter of fact, he should do no such thing, for a busy man in dictating letters will often be guilty of errors which would make his letter ridiculous if it were written just as he dictated it." [12] Moreover, the secretary should be sure that his employer worked systematically. "This he can usually do by first planning the system for his employer and then getting him to adopt it unconsciously. . . . It is the secretary's duty to keep after his employer so that he does his work, but there is, of course, great need for tact and diplomacy in getting the employer to adopt a system." [13]

Secretaries were encouraged to organize their own work schedule, as well as that of their employers: "you must . . .

take an intelligent attitude toward the planning of your work. You are not told by your employer in just what order or at just what hours you should put through the work he places in your hands. You cannot turn to ask him 'What shall I do next?' You must turn to yourself with that question, and you must answer it with good judgment."[14] On the whole, private secretaries were being encouraged to think for themselves, at a time when principles of scientific management were imposing more and more control over lower-level clerical workers.

Secretarial work also encompassed a large variety of tasks. In 1910 one writer found it "difficult to imagine a profession less controlled by routine than that of a private secretary. Each day differs from the preceding one, and there is never a dull succession of drab weeks. Instead, the brain is kept alert by the questions and perplexities of the hour, and the ability to perform the daily duties 'judgmatically' grows with the months and years of experience."[15] Another study concluded that all the secretaries shared "the unshakeable belief that her particular job was absolutely unique and that the information she gave could scarcely be helpful as it was not representative."[16] That secretaries believed in the uniqueness of their individual job suggests that secretarial work did indeed vary a good deal, and that many tasks common to all secretaries could be combined in an infinite number of ways.

Charters and Whitley seem to have been the first to undertake a systematic investigation of these tasks. They found that "the median number of duties performed by an individual was about 130 with three-fourths of the secretaries performing less than 210 duties each."[17] Of the 130 tasks most frequently performed, over sixty involved correspondence and writing. Twenty-five fell into the category of a general knowledge of office procedure; fourteen were concerned with the physical maintenance of the office; fifteen involved the secretary acting as the personal emissary or extension of the employer, answering the telephone, greeting callers, even "getting rid of cranks and beggars"; ten covered the organization of the office work

—the secretary's, the employer's, or that of other office workers; while only three fell into the category of personal errands for the employer.

This breakdown seems to indicate that almost half of the tasks the average secretary did involved correspondence and writing. In compiling their list of secretarial duties, however, Charters and Whitley made a more detailed breakdown in these areas than in others. For example, they separated "open mail" and "seal mail," as well as a large variety of intermediate steps such as "fold letters" and "insert letters in envelopes." But when the secretary acted as the employer's personal emissary, they only listed "meet callers," omitting "bid farewell to callers," which might be seen as analogous to "seal mail." Thus it is difficult to determine precisely what proportion of their time secretaries devoted to various tasks.

Nonetheless, the complexity of secretarial work certainly emerges. It is possible to determine what percentage of the secretaries studied by Charters and Whitley were performing the various duties. For instance, 84 percent said that they composed letters on their own, while only 70 percent indicated that they sharpened their own pencils. Sixty-two percent made engagements or appointments for their employers, but only 50 percent ran errands. And more secretaries (42 percent) took care of flowers than planned work for others (37 percent). Some of this variance may have been due to office size. In a large office, where there were enough workers to merit a division of labor, one employee might well sharpen all the pencils, clean and oil typewriters, be responsible for office supplies and for locking desks and safes, and so on, thus relieving the private secretaries of those tasks. The literature on secretarial work stresses the ability to write some of the employer's business correspondence. In 1917 one author concluded, "the writing of letters is probably the most common duty of secretaries. . . . The employer may be an excellent letter writer, but he seldom has time to dictate word for word each letter that leaves the office."[18] This commentator also described the situation of Frank Campbell, a secretary who received a telegram from his "chief," saying that he would not return from his weekend in the country until late Tuesday afternoon, and that in the meantime a speech on bonus systems should be prepared for him.

> At five o'clock [on Monday afternoon] Campbell was back at the office. He cleaned up the few remaining business matters of the day and departed for home—and work, for he had to write the speech that night if it were to be done at all.
>
> It was late that night before Frank Campbell had finished the skeleton outline and the rough draft of the speech, but the sound sleep, induced partly by fatigue and partly by the consciousness of work well done, left him much refreshed the next morning.
>
> Mr. Forbes did not arrive at four o'clock as he had telegraphed Campbell. But at 5:30 he walked rapidly into the office and greeted the somewhat worried Campbell.
>
> "I was detained by a tire blow-out," panted Mr. Forbes. "Must hurry along and get dressed. Is the speech ready?"
>
> "Yes, sir," said Campbell. He reached into the desk drawer, pulled out the typewritten speech and the outline which he had typed on the note cards. These he handed to his chief, who hurriedly glanced through the material, nodded to himself once or twice, and then rushed out of the office, stuffing the sheets into the pocket of his duster.
>
> When Mr. Forbes arrived at the office at 9:15 Wednesday morning, he first answered the greeting of his secretary and then said, "The talk made quite a hit last night. But where did you get such good ideas?"[19]

Writing tasks went with the job. A secretary was expected to know how to take dictation, transcribe shorthand notes into a written text, use the typewriter accurately and quickly, and be able to compose letters and documents. But there was other work as well: The secretary was expected to be familiar with the entire office routine.

> An accurate *typist* can copy legal documents without error. A well-trained *switchboard operator* can handle many active lines at

once. A superior *dictating machine operator* can transcribe evenly and well from successive records. A competent *bookkeeper* can be relied on for correct accounts. But a secretary must expect to be doing, watching, thinking, talking, listening, starting this, finishing that, waiting, co-operating. And all these activities will be bound up in tasks very different from one another in kind and in importance and in length of time required for their completion.[20]

A private secretary was expected to have a thorough knowledge of the filing system, although the actual filing might be done by others. "Also, he will give directions, even though he does not file letters himself, as to how certain letters are to be filed."[21] Nor was the secretary limited to the details of office procedure; he or she might well be "called upon to advise with his executive in large questions of policy. Since this is so, the private secretary, besides having a knowledge of the duties of a private secretary, should have a sound, broad knowledge of business in general and a specific knowledge of the particular business of the employer."[22] This was often true of private secretaries to professionals, especially in a relatively small office. Thus the duties of a physician's secretary were said to include receiving patients, making engagements, answering the telephone, keeping accounts and records of patients, aiding in the editing of medical publications, assisting in laboratory analysis, and helping, under direction, in minor operations.[23] A secretary in a law firm was accountable for "all kinds of systematic filing, clerical office work, accounting, private correspondence, library work, court reporting, and executive supervision of a staff of clerical assistants and office routine."[24]

While a general knowledge of office procedure might involve the secretary in such exalted tasks as "advising with the executive in matters of policy" and supervising other office workers, he or she was also expected to take a part in physically maintaining the office. By 1940 a writer assumed that private secretaries were women, and advised them that they would be expected to inject a "woman's touch" in the office. She took it for granted that a woman would know better than her male boss how "to hang pictures or to pick a suitable spot on the wall for his pet wall-eyed pike." They could also arrange flowers artistically if they were lucky enough to work for a man who liked them. However, secretaries were urged to "remember that the majority of offices are the bailiwicks of men, not women, and ruffles and kindred frills are taboo."[25]

The secretary was also required to be a personal emissary or extension of the employer, and thus might make appointments or even serve as the employer's conscience when he was tempted to stray from the dictates of proper business behavior. "The secretary should strive to prevent his employer from breaking an engagement. It is better for the secretary to incur the displeasure of his chief for the time being, so long as he gets him to keep the appointment."[26]

Secretaries were also often advised to get to know their employers as well as possible, so that they would be familiar with their every personal preference, and would be able to "put themselves in their employer's shoes" in their absence. Thus the model secretary was "to find out how the employer wants everything done and then to act in that way"—in effect to be an extension of the employer. The secretary should even learn about "the friends and acquaintances of the employer and about the important callers at the office. . . . The secretary will soon learn, for example, which friend is to have the right of way in luncheon engagements, who has the privilege of walking unannounced into the private office, and so on. The secretary, moreover, should strive to get into the good graces of his employer's friends."[27]

The organization and supervision of office practices, still another category of secretarial work, was one more way in which secretaries functioned as an extension of the employer. In supervising other office workers, they were operating as delegates or representatives of their employers. While overseeing other office workers was not a primary secretarial task, it was a responsibility for some. One writer found the secretary an important liaison between (male) employers and (female) office workers. This "trouble-shooter" should be "someone who has been through the mill herself and understands the problems of the girls: someone able to estimate how much work a girl should be able to turn out in a day and how much work each man in the office has to do." [28]

Secretarial work also included personal business and errands for the employers. Again not a priority, this was nonetheless part of the job. It covered making hotel and train reservations; handling money, which might well involve handling the employer's personal as well as business finances; depositing, writing, and cashing checks; and taking care of the check book and bank book. Personal errands were not a major portion of secretarial work, but they still rankled:

> One girl has to amuse her employer's two children every Saturday morning. It's a great day—for the kids. Distinguished visitors are apt to be hit in the eye with a misdirected ball, books are dragged from the shelves to build houses on the floor, but still the routine of the office must run smoothly on. The secretary is a capable young woman and usually manages to greet a caller and at the same time graciously kick a train of cars from before his feet. She can remove a regiment of soldiers from a chair even as she waves a guest into it, and playing horse with a rope around her waist and "Git up!" yelled in her ear, does not prevent her from calmly answering the phone and even typing an occasional letter.
>
> But one day when she found an eight-year-old crawling over her desk, his feet dragging over her neat pile of papers into ruin, she spanked him!
>
> No, she didn't lose her job. She's too valuable. [29]

In addition to minding employers' children, secretaries fetched and fixed their lunches, shopped for their gifts, and even ran errands for their wives.

In all of these aspects of the job, the secretary was expected to demonstrate initiative, to do the things that needed to be done without always asking permission. Such a secretary was a far cry from the lower-level clerical worker of scientific man-

agement, who was expected to execute a small number of routinized tasks at a fixed speed. Secretaries were expected to
think, and to understand how their responsibilities fit into the
entire business operation.

The Private Secretary as Buffer

The private secretary in effect served as a buffer between the
employer and the outside world. Acting as the personal emissary of the employer, he or she handled callers and regulated
their access to the employer; undertook personal errands and
protected him from involvement in the minutiae of daily life;
and "learned the ropes" of the businesses and bureaucracies to
be dealt with, thereby saving him from having to concern himself with large numbers of mundane albeit important details.
The point here is not that the secretary enabled his or her employer to become an ivory-tower recluse. Rather, the secretary
enabled him to conserve his energy. Protected from distractions and mundane tasks, he was thus free to do the "important" work and to make the "important" decisions.

According to a monograph of the Federal Board for Vocational Education, "the trained secretary relieves the executive
of all detail by keeping him informed as to the important hap-
penings in the business world that may be of particular interest . . . by gathering data for the preparation of papers and
speeches, by standing between him and the public . . . and in
every way by keeping the executive's time for the more important managerial responsibilities devolving upon him." [30] In one
1934 survey of secretarial traits and duties, both employers
and secretaries ranked "handle callers" in the most important
class of duties. Many offices were designed so that the private
secretary's desk was adjacent to the employer's office. Thus
stationed, he or she could intercept callers, deciding whether
to turn them away, ask them to wait, or usher them into the

employer's office; could take phone calls and decide whether or not to transfer the call to the employer. One book devoted an entire chapter to the subject of "Managing Callers":

> The secretary meets and manages callers. The correct perfor-
> mance of this duty is important because it means a saving of from
> one to three hours each day in the executive's time—hours that
> can easily be wasted if every caller at the office is granted admit-
> tance to the chief. Again, the employer will be subjected to many
> annoyances, worries, and disagreeable experiences if beggars,
> cranks, and others of such types are freely admitted. This duty of
> acting as buffer between the employer and the caller is difficult,
> for it involves the exercise of great tact and discretion on the part
> of the secretary if he is to be at all successful. The secretary, in
> other words, must be able to "meet the people." [31]

The author explained in detail how to distinguish between important and unimportant calls, stressed the importance of courtesy to all callers, and described how to pull an employer away from overlong calls. The entire chapter aims at safeguarding an employer's time and, toward this end, is willing to contemplate duplicity. Thus it suggests that all callers be given appointments for the following day. The employer could then look over this schedule and decide which ones to keep. Should cancellation be in order, then "the secretary can say that 'Mr. Harrow was unexpectedly called away and will be unable to see you until next week,' or, 'Mr. Harrow is still busy on the matter he was working on yesterday and will be unable to see you,' or some other reason can be given." [32]

The secretary can screen telephone calls and transfer only those calls deemed of sufficient importance. He or she might also place calls for the employer, thereby sparing him the tedium of waiting for the person called to get on the line. This sometimes led to secretaries jousting for their respective employers:

> In certain cases where both men concerned are important men,
> the secretary of each will try to get the other principal to the

'phone before his own chief takes the phone. Secretaries do this in order that they may save their own employers the trouble of saying, "Hello, Mr. Blank?" and of then finding out that the person talking at the other end of the wire is Mr. Blank's secretary.

In some cases the battle of wits between the two secretaries, each striving to get the other man on the wire before he puts his own employer on, *lasts for four or five minutes.* Various subterfuges and stratagems are used. One secretary will say, "Yes, Mr. Smith is here and is ready to talk. Put your chief on," The other secretary will say: "Just a minute"—and then a few seconds later will say, "Hello, is this Mr. Smith?" hoping that in the meanwhile the other secretary will have put on her own chief. As a rule, however, where the employers are of about the same importance in business, the secretary who is calling up the other man should give in.[33]

The secretary was "the gateway to the employer," according to one writer. "If the gate swings easily, a man or woman glides into his or her appointment with the employer's interview already well begun. And it is fully as important that, if you can meet people with understanding, you will be able to turn away those whom your employer *refuses* to see, and with a grace that does not send them away 'queered.'"[34] Another observer considered that part of a secretary's job even included protection from the "female vamp."

"It's part of my business," said the attractive young woman in charge of a physician's office, "to have plenty of errands which take me into the room where the doctor has a woman patient. I keep going in and out and leave the door open behind me. You should see the looks I get sometimes! But the doctor asks me to do it. It's part of my job.

"You would be surprised at the things women will do when they want to get a man. And if the door is shut, even if everything is as proper as an interview with [Herbert] Hoover, they can go away and tell anything they want to about what has happened. But with me in the room half the time it's hard to get by with anything, even a story."[35]

Thus did the private secretary act as intermediary and as buffer. Consequently he or she was endowed with considerable authority, and could determine whether a caller merited attention and, to a certain degree, whether the employer should be exposed to his callers. Furthermore, by seeming to require a buffer, an employer's importance was enhanced. He was indeed an important person, whose time was far too valuable to be wasted on such details as arranging an appointment or dialing a telephone. His secretary, conversely, being less important, could spend his or her less valuable time on just such trivia.

Even writing doggerel for the employer to send to his sweetheart might be included among secretarial responsibilities:

> Your eyes are stars of the summer night,
>> Your cheeks are a pair of roses,
> Your lips—well, I'd be happy quite
>> If they were where my nose is.

"That's the best I can do," growled the harassed-looking man, tearing a sheet of paper from his typewriter. "Let the old man do his own stuff."

The other men in the office grinned in sympathy. They had all been at it, the past week, writing poetry for the boss. You see, the chief had a sweetheart who demanded a fresh stanza dedicated to her charms every day. But he had gone away on a vacation and, wishing to have perfect rest, had left the poetry job to his secretary. For the first week the secretary kept up under the strain, but after that she had to call in outside help, and all the men in the office had taken a hand at it.

"I really wasn't hired to write verses to his lady friends!" exclaimed the secretary in some indignation.

Well, perhaps not. But there are a lot of things, as this girl discovered, which a secretary does for her employer that are not mentioned when she takes the job. It's something like a bride on her wedding day. She doesn't get the idea when the organ is throbbing with the strains of "Oh, Promise Me," that "Love, honor and obey" is going to mean hunting collar buttons and washing the baby's clothes. Neither does the secretary always realize, when she is en-

gaged at thirty-five per, that she may be asked to do almost anything for her employer, from picking out his tie to buying his wife's
birthday present.[36]

There are comparable examples. One secretary was expected
to help out an employer with his current love affair. She "was
familiar with the whole thing, knew the lady well, ordered her
daily flowers, and helped select her presents." The employer
even solicited advice from his secretary when he wanted to
break off the affair.[37] More frequently, the secretary was directed to buy gifts for wives and friends of the employer. One
confidential secretary, describing her rise to this lofty position,
noted: "I had also begun to execute all sorts of personal mis-
sions for Mr. Blank. I did considerable banking and made numerous purchases of various kinds, even Christmas presents
when that season rolled around."[38] In the survey of valued secretarial duties and traits, employers stated: "she had kept track
of my Christmas list for me from the previous year"; "she
keeps me from going home empty-handed on birthdays and
anniversaries."[39]

Secretaries not only bought gifts for their employers' wives.
They also ran errands for them. One secretary was fired because she refused to run any more.

A scrap of silk was the final straw that broke the camel's back.
One bitter day in February, when a driving sleet was fairly rattling
the windowpanes, she called up and asked me to match some
samples at a Fifth Avenue shop near Fiftieth Street. She apolo-
gized for asking me to go out on such a dreadful day by explaining
that she hated to take the limousine out in such weather! I know
that this sounds incredible, but it is the simple truth.

The errand meant a trip of at least an hour and a half. My desk
was piled with work that must be finished in time to catch the last
mail. Even if I cut my lunch hour short, I would have to strain
every nerve in order to clear my desk by five o'clock.

I thought of these things, but somehow I couldn't bring myself
to use them as an excuse. I simply said that I was sorry, but that I
would be unable to match the samples for Mrs. Brown on that or

any other day. She was as surprised as if I had struck her. No doubt she thought me a monster of ingratitude.

The next day happened to be Saturday. When I opened my pay envelope, I found two weeks' salary and notice that my services would not be further required.[40]

Nor was it unusual for a secretary to be asked to fix food for the employer, and sometimes to share it with him. Lauretta Fancher cited the case of a secretary in Philadelphia whose boss was a "food crank" and who joined him in a regular lunch of lettuce and milk.[41] Another "used to make milk toast for his breakfast. . . . No matter what was going on, I had to drop everything at eleven o'clock in the morning and again at three in the afternoon, and trot out for his glass of milk and plate of graham crackers."[42]

Secretaries often did their employers' personal banking. One employer, when asked what secretaries had done for him that "pleased him very much," answered, "She handles my personal checking account. I never can make it come out even, but she fixes it up—I think a girl should know something about banking."[43]

Most of the evidence about the personal errands that secretaries ran for their employers comes from accounts written by secretaries themselves about the ups and downs of their work. These stories, published in such popular magazines as *Collier's*, *Ladies Home Journal*, and *American Magazine*, provide a colorful glimpse of what a few secretaries, at least, thought about their jobs. One subject that figured prominently in those thoughts was running personal errands for the boss, and resenting it. Employers, on the other hand, placed very little emphasis on personal errands. In fact, the only ones that they mentioned were personal banking and gift buying. This is hardly surprising: the employer who demanded his milk and crackers at eleven every morning was not too likely to brag about it.

Such tasks were only the most prominent form of the personal errand. Dialing and answering the telephone, opening and sealing letters, even composing speeches and letters were all personal services performed as part of the secretary's job routine. These innumerable acts of minor servitude, rather than the less frequent present-buying, constituted the bulk of such errands and were at the heart of the division of labor between employer and personal secretary. They were so much taken for granted that they were seldom remarked upon by either in the literature on personal secretaries. They were a fundamental feature of office work, assumed as a given and passing without question.

The Personal Secretary as Servant

The very work of acting as buffers and of running errands casts light upon the objective place of private secretaries in the world of work. They were servants. Thus the literature places trust and deference high on the list of desired qualities.

In the first place, a secretary was supposed to defer to the opinions and judgments of his or her employer. "Adaptability" —"she puts up with the views of the individual above her to the point where it is quite against her own make-up"—and "personal pleasantness"—"she is not always determined to have her own way"—were stressed.[44] Sometimes deference had its limits. One secretary recalls:

> I started working for a Mr. Lyons, who owned a good-sized letter-shop. He wanted some one who, as soon as she was familiar with the work, could take charge of the office and the twenty-some girls who were doing the typing. He had spent four hours in interviewing me to make sure I was the right person. The first morning he handed me the checks to make the deposit and suddenly screamed: "Look at them, look at them, look at them!"
>
> "I *am* looking at them," I said.
>
> "Now, that won't do," he said. "I may be snappy, but it doesn't mean you have done anything. I have a great deal on my mind."

I laughed and said: "Well, if you are snappy without cause, I'll certainly say something back."

"No. That won't do."

It was eleven o'clock when I left. I had worked two hours.[45]

But this same woman chose subservience with another employer when, working as a bookkeeper, she was asked to get a feather duster for the office.

"A cloth is much better," I said.

"What?" the president said. "We always did have a feather duster."

When the president left the room, I said to the secretary: "Does he really want a feather duster?"

"Sure. He always used to have a feather duster. He likes to slap it around in those file-boxes on top of the desks and make the dust fly over everything. When he gets started with a feather duster the dust rises up in clouds thick enough to choke you."[46]

She bought the feather duster.

"Secretaries are actually glorified valets," one writer candidly observed. "They must know the meaning of personal service and what it means to a busy man. Naturally a man likes to have his wants attended to, who doesn't? You are in the office to serve your employer. Don't feel that you are too dignified or too well educated or too something else to serve him."[47]

Nonetheless, most writers acknowledged that there were times when deference was not in order—for instance, when the secretary knew that the employer was making an important mistake. Even then, however, diplomacy and tact were advised. The secretary, in making corrections, was still expected to defer to his or her employer's feelings and ego. When Gladys Torson suggested that secretaries try to break their employers of "bad business habits," she warned that since "no one likes to think that he is being reformed . . . any measures you take will have to be diplomatic."[48] In a chapter entitled "Soothing the Tired Business Man," she offers the following example of how the good secretary catered to her boss's psyche:

> At first the man was inclined not to like his new secretary; he thought she was too mouselike, but he soon found out what a joy it was to have someone walk quietly into the room, answer him in a soft voice, and sit in the chair without squirming while he dictated. He could splutter and mutter as much as he liked but his secretary only smiled sympathetically, as though that were the way a man is supposed to act in an office. She didn't force her personality into the picture (yes, she had one, too) and gradually the man's nervous tension began to relax.
>
> "I don't know she's there, most of the time," he said, "and yet I feel confident that she is getting down what I am saying, that she understands me and sympathizes with me and my problems. I've been a different man since she came to work for me. She doesn't act as though she thought she was smarter than I am. Maybe she is, I shouldn't be surprised, but I have to think I'm smart these days or I couldn't hold my own in business."[49]

Deference included being a good listener. "Every secretary who ever pounded the keys," one writer concluded, "will admit that there are times when she has had to be a safety valve. And a sponge. Listen when he feels like talking. Absorb, sympathize. And keep her mouth shut."[50] Sooner or later, she noted, most employers got around to complaining about the fact that "their wives did not understand them," while the secretary lent a sympathetic ear. Another observer, in agreement, blamed their wives: *I wish the boss's wife would listen when he wants to talk about himself.* Apparently she doesn't, for I have to spend half an hour every day listening to what he did and said about things I already know by heart."[51]

Most studies of clerical labor comment on this pattern of subservience and enlarge on it. The authors of *Secretarial Efficiency* admonished secretaries "to acquire skill in carrying through work not in a go-as-you-please manner but in a go-as-your-employer-pleases manner."[52] As far as the author of "How

I Became a Confidential Secretary" was concerned, this was the essential difference between a stenographer and a secretary. "The former makes herself and her work the dominant features, while to the latter her employer, his requirements and his characteristics are the chief end and aim of her thought. She subjugates her own personality in every sense of the word; yet she is not servile."[53] Remarkably enough, one of the examples that the secretaries in the Charters and Whitley study gave for what they meant by the trait "intelligence" was the ability to "always put self in employer's position and get his point of view."[54]

Deference could go well beyond catering to an employer's opinions, feelings, and peccadilloes. It might even involve the sacrifice of a personal life for the job. "Personal pleasantness," a desirable job trait, meant that a secretary could "put aside her own plans and do good work even though disappointed because they fell through." "Willingness" included "sacrifices personal interests to the good of the organization."[55] Indeed secretaries were expected to make virtually every aspect of their personal lives secondary:

> Since the secretary spends more than two-thirds of her time away from the office, what can she do about planning those hours intelligently to serve her secretarial efficiency as a whole? She can establish regular habits for exercise, sleep, recreation including reading, and for any home responsibilities she may have to carry. She must balance the budget of her time as she balances the budget of her money. If a secretary spends all her free time reading magazines, or attending the movies, or taking hard exercise, her expenditure of time is as poorly balanced as if she spent all her money on clothes. The time that is at your personal disposal should be enjoyed as a change from work. As to friends, amusements, sports—*choose whatever will combine to make you worth the most to your employer.*[56]

The duty of secretaries was to serve their employers, and in this respect they became servants. Not only were they to take dictation, answer the telephone, and perform the myriad other duties that came with the job; they had also been hired to serve—to cater to their employer's feelings and whims.

As well as deference, trustworthiness was of critical importance. It meant the ability to keep a secret, and included using deception, if that were the only way to avoid disclosure of private affairs: "Although the secretary has certain information and although he realizes that his questioner knows that he has the information," one observer wrote, "it is common practice for him to say that he does not know."[57] There was, another writer declared, "an unwritten code of high honor among true secretaries as to the privacy of their knowledge; they do not entertain their friends or their families with what does not belong to them."[58] The author of "The College Woman as Secretary," claimed that the most important qualification that a secretary could have was "character," which included "trustworthiness" and a "fine sense of honor."[59] Still another study prized "reticence"—which meant that the secretary was "careful about mentioning business affairs in public places where people overhearing might make use of information."[60]

"Honesty" was also highly regarded among secretarial qualities. It covered such actions as not appropriating "office supplies for personal use," "doing an honest day's work—that is, she does not loaf on the job, but gives full value for what she receives," and not concealing "information the employer should have."[61] Honesty included not taking bribes:

> it would certainly be a betrayal of trust to accept these small bribes to do that which the secretary would not otherwise do. . . . The secretary should avoid accepting the gifts, if he can. But if he finds that it is impossible under the conditions to refuse the small gift or to send it back, he should keep it with the idea fully known that it is not in any way to influence him to favorable action for the giver.[62]

Loyalty to the "chief," after all, was primary. A secretary could "be friendly with all the [office] girls but not too intimate with any of them."[63] She was expected to sacrifice any potentially close friendships with other office workers so that her employer would not doubt that her primary loyalty lay with him.

Private secretaries, behaving as trustworthy personal servants, often functioned as extensions of their employers. They did the detail work, the trivia, but they might also be expected to direct and supervise other office workers. In his study of the duties and traits of the personal secretary, Nichols defined "executive ability." It consisted "not only in directing detail work but in acting directly for, or in place of, her chief."[64] Another study provided a list describing the secretary with "executive ability":

> she can get work out of people without friction
> she can administer the details of the office
> she can "boss" when necessary—that is, give people the impression of authority
> she is not so easy on her subordinates that they take advantage of it
> she plans work for the others in the office
> she makes the work run according to schedule and without confusion
> she handles the personnel problems that come up in the office in the way most conducive to harmony
> she gets direct action on matters that come up
> she supervises the office work
> she employs assistants[65]

Not all secretaries had "to answer questions or decide matters for other members of the office force," as Charters and Whitley put it. Indeed, a majority of the secretaries they interviewed did not. But forty percent did:

> Six said they had to decide matters of punctuation, spelling, sentence construction, the form of letters, etc., for stenographers and clerks. Three had to distribute work among the other members of the staff. Nineteen directed the work of one typist or stenographer, who asked questions with regard to all phases of office work. Eight secretaries planned the work of two stenographers and answered all their queries. Two secretaries planned the work of three girls,

two supervised five girls, one had charge of six stenographers, one had charge of fourteen girls, and one supervised all female employees of the organization, which necessitates settling disputes of various kinds, answering questions, and so on.[66]

Emphasis was placed on the secretary's appearance and personality. Because secretaries were an extension of the employer, how they looked and behaved reflected directly on him. The gracious secretary would "give the impression to callers that no matter how trifling the interview might be I should have been glad to have seen them if at all possible"; "make people feel that she is doing a lot for them"; and "smooth people over when they are irritated." And "tact" marked the secretary who did "not offend queer people by in any way emphasizing or calling attention to their queerness," and did not remind "poor patients . . . of their poverty in any way."[67]

In 1924 one writer indicated that male and female secretaries differed in the ability to make their personalities reflect well on their employers:

In so far as any general statement can be true, male secretaries are more likely not to possess suitable manners than are female secretaries; perhaps because it is man's nature to be more unrestrained and more independent than women, perhaps because men are not so sensitive to the effects of manners as women are and hence do not appreciate their value. It is a fact, moreover, that some male secretaries at the beginning of their work feel that it is unmanly, a sign of effeminacy, and affected to show to a caller, for example, such little attentions and civilities as asking him whether he will have a chair, and whether he would not care to look at a magazine while he is waiting to see the chief. Some male secretaries have the belief that it is businesslike to be curt and brusque in their speech and actions; that in this democratic country everybody is equal and that therefore they need not show proper deference to superiors, older persons, and women; and that, in general, gentility in manners is an indication of weakness and not becoming to a real man. If a secretary has such beliefs and if he acts according to them, he will soon learn his mistakes. Not only will a disregard of manners offend callers and others who come in contact with the secretary, but crude manners will create a poor impression of the chief. . . .

Women secretaries, although they know as only women can know the value of manners, often have the faults nonetheless of being careless in observing the amenities of the position and indifferent to the necessity of putting themselves out to accommodate callers at the office.[68]

Although indicating that the manners of a female secretary better represented her employer than did those of a male, the author was not one to say that women were preferable to men as private secretaries.

Appearance was as important as personality. One writer cautioned male secretaries that "slovenly, careless attire is a great handicap. Odd, ill-fitting clothes and flashy or sporty dress are offensive to good taste. The best way to dress is in such conformity with convention that the dress arouses no unfavorable comment. . . . As [the secretary] knows that his dress will not be an object of criticism, he is not afraid to go among important people."[69] The author of *The Efficient Secretary* advised women secretaries neither to underdress nor overdress. Women, he cautioned,

are apt to wear fluffy, frilly, chiffon-like garments and unnecessary furbelows, or they are apt to fly to the other extreme and dress in tweeds and cheviots, cut in masculine lines.

That the first extreme mentioned is never in good taste and never permissible for business wear goes without saying. The latter is permissible, to be sure, but unbecoming, except when worn by a woman who is dainty, girlish, and very feminine. When worn by a woman who is at all large or ungraceful, dress tending toward masculinity increases the appearance of ungainliness.[70]

This last comment suggests that at times private secretaries were seen as extensions of the office furniture as well as of their employers, valued for their decorative effect. In one study, a definition of "attractive personal appearance" includes "she must look like a lady: I don't want her painted, rouged, perfumed to such an extent that it will be an offense to me and my patients. She should dress like a lady, not extreme silk stockings, and high-heeled shoes." It emphasized "grooming": "her clothes are in good repair, not in obvious need of mending, with hooks and eyes and buttons missing, lace torn, trimming partly ripped off, etc." [71] The author of "One Secretary as per Specifications" was most explicit on the importance of a secretary's decorative value:

> The telephone tinkles. The clerk holds the French instrument to her ear with her left hand and writes down the incoming order with her right:
>
> "An exceptionally attractive, intelligent young woman, not over twenty-five; must be educated and well bred, with charming personality; a natural blonde, five feet eight inches tall, and slender; a smart wardrobe necessary."
>
> Laying down specifications very much as he would for a yacht, Charles Hewling Ballinger, vice president of Mastings and Co., automobile manufacturers, is ordering a secretary. [72]

The decorative function, mentioned only in connection with female secretaries, was denied by some: "The duties of a private secretary have been gilded to such an extent by the popular novelists and playwrights that the prevailing idea among the uninitiated is that letter-writing in a fair hand constitutes the most difficult of the tasks imposed, and that, when not occupied with correspondence, the secretary stands in effective attitudes in a more or less well-lighted background. However familiar this may be in theory, practice speedily pinpricks this peaceful and alluring bubble." [73] The writer then went on to explain how complex and demanding the work actually was. It would be hard to determine if many secretaries were, in fact, hired primarily on the basis of their personal attractiveness, as Elizabeth Ragan suggested. That the subject came up at all indicates that a secretary's appearance was of *some* importance. Understandably so, since a secretary's attractiveness reflected well on the employer—he had an attractive extension of himself in the office. Then, too, some employers found a certain amount of sexual gratification in having attractive women around them. Finally, as the job became identified with women, there was mention in the literature of the secretary as the "office wife." This at a time when wives were still thought of as extensions and reflections of their husbands.

> A man chooses his secretary much as he chooses his wife, and for much the same reasons. She looks good to him. He sees a slim, engaging young woman with a frank smile and readiness to approve of him, who yet retains a wholesome respect for her own qualifications, and he decides instantly: "That's my secretary." The alliance—shall we say business love at first sight?—works about as marriages do.[74]

As this writer points out, the "office wife" was valued not only for her appearance, although it may have had much to do with why she initially was hired. She was also expected to be competent, enhancing her attractiveness with efficiency. Arguing that the actual wives may not have been doing their jobs well, one author believed that "every man needs a woman's tenderness and her pride and faith in his ability, to buck him up in the fight he must make in these days of terrific competition."[75] Another secretary, concurring with this ideal, provided a remarkable set of parallels between the "office wife" and the actual wife:[76]

TO PRODUCE SATISFACTORY RESULTS, THE SECRETARY AS WELL AS THE HOUSEKEEPER HAS TO COMBINE SKILL AND KNOWLEDGE WITH HER PERSONAL TRAITS

The Housekeeper Must	*The Secretary Must*
Understand and take efficient care of kitchen equipment	Understand and take efficient care of office equipment
Understand varied domestic skills	Understand varied secretarial skills
Know how to follow a detailed recipe in the right order	Know how to follow detailed instructions in the right order

The Housekeeper Must	*The Secretary Must*
Give attention to her work—often to several tasks at once	Give attention to her work—often to several tasks at once
Be willing to carry through minor duties, especially the monotonous ones and those that do not show how much work is involved	Be willing to carry through minor duties, especially the monotonous ones and those that do not show how much work is involved
Buy supplies economically	Buy supplies economically
Keep materials in convenient order for ready use	Keep supplies ready at her employer's and her own desk
Make every motion count	Make every motion count
Know how to plan and carry out every detail of getting a meal so that it is all ready at the right time	Know how to plan and carry out every detail of the day's work and the week's work so that tasks are finished on time
Know how to use the odds and ends of food	Know how to use the odds and ends of time and supplies
Understand the tastes of the family	Understand the personal requirements of her employer
Make food attractive	Put through neat, well-arranged work
Be able to cooperate with others	Be able to cooperate with others
Be patient with interruption	Be patient with interruption
Know how to telephone courteously but firmly if there is an error in an order	Know how to telephone courteously but firmly if there is an error in an order

Casting the private secretary as the "office wife" was in some ways the ultimate in making secretaries surrogates for their employers. After all, the general cultural assumption had it that a wife was a loyal extension of her husband. The characterization of the private secretary as the "office wife" implied that her loyalty to her boss was similar to that of a wife to her husband. Certainly, nowhere was it recognized that an employer and his paid worker, the private secretary, might have conflicting interests.

Private secretarial work by its nature endowed secretaries with knowledge about, and, consequently, power within, their offices. Instead of being restricted to a narrow range of tasks, as lower-level clerical workers were, private secretaries were in a position to know a great deal about all that went on in their office. Relatively free to acquire knowledge about the workings of an office, and encouraged to take on as many responsibilities as they could handle, secretaries were often in a potentially powerful position. Their knowledge of the office and its procedures enabled them to manipulate those procedures if they so desired. For example, a departmental secretary in a university, familiar with the institution's operations, might be aware that the important person to speak to about financial aid was the *assistant* to the director of the Financial Aid Office. For she would know that the assistant really made all the final decisions, since the director spent his time doing outside fundraising for the university. Or a secretary in an insurance company might be acquainted with the head of the mail room, and would use that personal relationship to have mail shipments delayed until her last-minute letters could get into the day's mail. In addition to this ability to manipulate office procedures, secretaries had the power to control, to a certain extent, the contacts between their employers and the outside world. Presumably secretaries followed their employers' general wishes in screening callers, but nonetheless their position as guardians of the gate gave them some control over the employers themselves. Secretaries also had the power to withhold their work. "I know a secretary who does the right thing by her boss's letters *except on days when she is annoyed with him.* On those days, which fortunately aren't frequent, she transcribes material exactly as it is dictated to her. Having seen some of her transcriptions on these 'off' days, I told her this seemed like a terrible revenge."[77]

The private secretary certainly had more power in the office than the lower-level clerical workers. But it was a power that went largely unrecognized. As Frances Faunce put it, "the combined details of what a secretary attends to often have a far-reaching effect, but they seldom bear her name. They are a part of what may be called the 'secret service' of the profession. It is like team-work that does not care so much who makes the goals as how many are made by the team."[78] Such anonymity was rarely rewarded. At times the value of a private secretary was publicly recognized, but that did not mean promotion, though the secretary might have all the credentials for the opening. In fact, a secretary's competence and power were usually recognized only in well-worn office folklore. Thus an employer would introduce his private secretary as "Miss Brown. She *really* runs things around here." (Laughter from all parties.) This remark may have been pretty close to the truth, but making it a joke diminished the secretary's real importance.

The private secretary's position as a buffer between the employer and the details of the outside world served to enhance the employer's importance and to reinforce the hierarchy within the office. Indeed, when performing essentially personal services such as dialing the telephone for the employer, the secretary was acting as his servant. This reinforced the notion that those people at the top of the office hierarchy, who merited such a servant, were different and more important than those at the bottom, who did not. Other aspects of the office hierarchy—such as the fact that those at the top were paid much more money than those at the bottom—were thereby justified. The deference that private secretaries were expected to show their employers also reinforced the office hierarchy. It not only underscored the employer's importance, but also belittled the secretaries' competence and knowledge, their judgment and opinions. It contributed to a state of affairs where private secretaries were paid much less than their employers and where promotions to managerial positions were very rare indeed. Thus deference not only made secretaries' knowledge and competence less important; it made *them* seem less important.

It is very hard to find any statistics exclusively about private secretaries.[79] For example, the comprehensive survey of the labor force, *Comparative Occupation Statistics for the United States, 1870 to 1940*, breaks down clerical occupations into the following categories: agents, collectors, and credit men; book-keepers, cashiers, and accountants; clerks "except 'clerks' in stores;" messenger, errand, and office boys and girls; and stenographers and typists.[80] Presumably, private secretaries were subsumed in one of these categories. Consequently, it is difficult to derive any information about differences between male and female secretaries. Two places where "private secretary" was treated as a separate category indicate that the overall feminization of clerical workers also applied to private secretaries. In 1902 only 34 percent of all Massachusetts private secretaries were women; in a 1926 survey the figure was 84 percent.[81]

Reluctance to hire females for clerical work in general spilled over into questions of their suitability as private secretaries. In 1910, for example, the secretary to the future Supreme Court Justice Louis D. Brandeis noted that "those women who are now filling positions as confidential secretaries are still considered something of an experiment, and there are many business men who have not yet grown sufficiently accustomed to placing confidence in a woman's discretion and ability to enable them to appreciate her possible worth in business and utilize her capabilities."[82]

The hesitations faded, however, as a growing number of women filled the positions. An advice handbook of 1917 was addressed exclusively to men; the 1924 edition was intended for both sexes. By the 1930s, the handbooks were being addressed exclusively to women: witness, for instance, Faunce and Nichols's *Secretarial Efficiency* (1939) and Gladys Torson's *"Ask My Secretary . . .": The Art of Being a Successful Business Girl* (1940).

The feminization of private secretaries can be accounted for as part of the trend toward feminization in clerical work as a whole. But other factors also help to explain the phenomenon. First, in a male-dominated society such as the United States, custom dictated that women should defer to the greater knowledge and better judgment of men. As has been noted, deference was an important aspect of the private secretary's job, and employers may have found that deference was easier to extract from a female private secretary than from a male. Second, female private secretaries were thought to be entirely satisfied with their position in life, and unlikely to aspire to managerial positions. An employer seeking someone permanent would try to find a woman, avoiding male applicants who might be moving on to bigger and better things. "In some offices," one writer stated, "the private secretary is an understudy of the chief and expects to be promoted to an executive position later. This is especially so where the secretary is a *man*. In other cases the private secretary is not being groomed for a more responsible position. *She* has achieved a permanent status which is entirely satisfactory to her. Increased financial rewards will be achieved through making herself more valuable to her employer and finding new ways to serve him efficiently and, for his point of view, profitably."[83] In 1921 the author of *Women Professional Workers* warned women that if they wanted to rise to management positions, they would do well to avoid secretarial ones. "The days are fast passing when the office boy, the junior clerk, or the stenographer with little education can forge ahead and become a manager or an official of the company." She advised women seeking business careers to "ask themselves whether secretarial training as now given is the best approach to management."[84]

There was, then, good reason why female private secretaries became the norm. In a society where it was assumed that women were not looking for important positions in the labor market, and that they worked only out of economic necessity or to mark time before marriage, the dead-end position of private secretary would seem perfectly adequate. For men, on the other hand, aspiring to rise in the labor market hierarchy, the position of private secretary would not seem ideal. Women made fine private secretaries because they should not and would not expect anything better; men, having greater expectations, did not. Or so the justification went.

The case of the private secretary shows that not all clerical work was subject to the kinds of degradation promoted by scientific office management, even though it is not clear that the private secretary's job required more skill than the pre–Civil War clerk's. Furthermore, many aspects of the private secretary's job show that the personal nature of the relationship between employer and employee in the office has not entirely disappeared. First of all, the very fact that the secretary was expected to behave as the employer's servant testifies to the personal relationship between the two. Second, personal secretary and employer were in essence sharing one job: the secretary did many of the minor, routine or menial tasks, while the employer's energies were saved for the creative, "important" aspects of the work. This division of labor between employer and secretary was often not a hard-and-fast affair. Instead, secretaries were encouraged to continually expand the scope of their duties, so that lines of demarcation between what was secretary's work and what was employer's were likely to be uncertain. This uncertainty would necessitate constant personal negotiation between employer and secretary.

Various aspects of the work and position of private secretaries distinguished them from other clerical workers. Several factors encouraged them to consider that their social and economic position derived primarily from the peculiarities of their individual job rather than from their membership in the clerical working class as a whole. The wide variety of tasks that were the province of the private secretary could be combined in an infinite number of ways. This encouraged private secretaries to think that their own particular job was unique and had little in common with the work of other private secretaries. Private secretaries who were expected to behave as servants towards their employers might well conclude that the characteristics of their work depended very heavily on the personal characteristics of their employer. A grouchy boss who treated his secretary like a doormat was likely to create a very different work atmosphere than the kindly executive who was willing to give his secretary a certain leeway in all sorts of matters, such as precisely when he or she arrived at and left work. Furthermore, their physical isolation from other office workers discouraged identification with them. The fact that private secretaries were expected to devote their primary loyalty to their employers, and that, as extensions of their employers, they were often put in positions of authority over other clerical workers only increased their isolation.

Still, one feature of private secretaries' work shows that they, too, were being proletarianized: the decline of promotional opportunities. Until about 1920, writings on private secretaries often mentioned that the job was good training for an executive position, implying that some private secretaries could make that upward move. But such talk faded after 1920. By the 1930s, some writers were even warning private secretaries, by now primarily women, that if they aspired to be executives, they should *not* start out as private secretaries. That job had now become the end of the line.

The feminization of private secretaries reinforced the notion that the job included being the employer's subordinate, the employee who performed the menial, routine and unimportant aspects of the work that they divided between them. In a patriarchal society it was natural that a male employer should give orders to and receive services from his female private secretary, and "natural" that, when a man and woman divided the work between them, the man should do all the creative, "important" parts and the woman all the routine, "unimportant" ones. Where a male executive commanded a male private secretary, there was potential for tension: the private secretary might resent being ordered about by another man, and an ambitious male private secretary might be champing at the bit to attain an executive position himself. Where a male employer commanded a female private secretary, such tensions were less likely. Not only was it "natural" for a woman to take orders from a man, but many women might not even aspire to an executive position, such a position being "unsuitable" for women. In this way the feminization of private secretaries was a stabilizing influence on the "proletarianization" of the position, and served to mute its impact.

8

Conclusion

The period from 1870 to 1930 witnessed profound changes in clerical work. By 1930 the fundamental characteristics that it still has today had been established. Clerical workers could be divided analytically into two basic groups: lower-level employees who executed routine tasks in a manner increasingly controlled and prescribed by employers; and, on a higher level best typified by private secretaries, those responsible for a wide variety of tasks who were encouraged to exercise a relatively greater degree of initiative and independence. Furthermore, clerical workers, who prior to 1870 had practically all been men, were by 1930 predominantly women. This feminization of the clerical labor force was related to the reorganization of clerical work.

Prior to 1870, offices were quite small, in general employing no more than a few clerks; consequently the division of clerical labor within them was rudimentary. Only four different kinds of employees can be distinguished—copyist, bookkeeper, office boy, and clerk. With the exception of the copyist who was hired purely to transcribe letters and other documents, these workers engaged in a wide variety of tasks and were able to learn a great deal about the workings of their firm. Furthermore, until at least the early nineteenth century, many clerks were specifically working as apprentices as a means of learning the business. After their apprenticeship, many went on to own and operate firms themselves. Much of the office work at this time was organized as an integrated whole—clerks were in a position not only to gain experience in the entire range of office work, but also to understand precisely how a particular task was related to overall office operations. Such employees were a far cry from scientifically managed clerical workers whose jobs had been reduced to the deadening repetition of a few steps in the labor process, and who had no opportunity to grasp how their tasks fit into the workings of the office on the whole.

Before 1870 relations between employer and employee were quite personal. That a clerkship was often seen as an apprenticeship meant that the employer often took a paternal role vis-a-vis his clerks. The small size of offices and the lack of codified bureaucratic procedures allowed an employer's personal idiosyncrasies to have a very large effect on the tenor of office relations. A harsh or ill-tempered employer could make life miserable for his clerks; with a lenient or kindly one things could be much more pleasant. Whether or not a clerk was trustworthy seems to have been very important to employers —an indication that they were forced to rely on the personal merits of their office help and were relatively unprotected by formal rules or bureaucratic procedures.

After 1870, however, political-economic changes had a profound effect on the organization of office work. Capitalist enterprises began to expand and to consolidate, resulting in much larger corporations whose operations covered a much wider geographic area. Moreover, other ancillary institutions expanded. Witness, for instance, the expansion in both size and scope of law offices, as well as municipal, state, and federal governments. Because of their need for more record-keeping and correspondence, these growing firms and institutions experienced a dramatic increase in the volume of office work. Naturally, the demand for office workers rose rapidly as well. This increasing need was the impetus for both the feminization and the reorganization of clerical work. Some employers soon found that in order to cope with the mounting paperwork, it was not sufficient merely to multiply the number of bookkeepers, copyists, office boys, and clerks. Furthermore, their burgeoning workforce was becoming more difficult to supervise. For both of these reasons, employers found it necessary to reorganize office work.

The primary characteristic of that reorganization was an elaboration of the division of labor, with the restructuring of firms into functionally defined departments being basic. The effect on clerical jobs was immediate. Confined to working in a single department, a clerical employee was now at best able to understand only how things were done in that one department. No longer was he or she doing a job whose vantage point afforded a picture of the entire operations of a firm. Departments were often divided and subdivided into their component parts, a process that served only to further the isolation of any single office job.

The scientific management of office work systematized the division and redivision of clerical labor. Although it was by no means universal, scientific management was in the vanguard of developments in office organization. Its two major characteristics were that each component step in the labor process should be executed using the cheapest possible labor, and that most clerical workers were to be divested of as much control as possible over their work, and relegated to the execution as opposed to the conception of their tasks. The first of these tenets was often termed "efficiency" by scientific managers, who thought it wasteful to expend the more highly paid labor of a "skilled" worker on a task which could just as easily be done by a lower-paid "unskilled" worker. But, as Harry Braverman has observed, the motive force behind the change was the drive for as much profit as possible, rather than some abstract concern for "efficiency."

The detailed division of labor was one of the ways in which scientific managers controlled clerical labor, for through its application they restricted the scope of clerical jobs and defined in very precise ways exactly what office workers were to do. Such restrictions further diminished the control that office workers exercised over their work. Placed in a position where they were unable to explore beyond the narrow confines of their individual jobs, and denied knowledge of how their own work fit into the firm's overall labor process, clerical workers could neither understand nor intelligently control their work.

Scientific management methods of control and supervision were not exclusively indirect or structural in chracter. Scientific managers dictated to the minutest degree imaginable the manner in which clerical workers were to execute their tasks; concocted a variety of premium and bonus schemes to induce their staff to produce up to and over the management-dictated standard; and arranged their offices so that employees would produce as much work and waste as little time as possible.

It is sometimes argued that machines caused the routinization of office work and the restriction of the office worker to a few limited tasks.[1] But nothing inherent in the typewriter, for instance, dictated that an individual clerical worker must operate it eight hours a day at a given rate of productivity. It was instead the particular organization of the office that tied an employee to the typewriter to the exclusion of any other duties. The successful invention and manufacture of the typewriter was a result of developments in the growth and organization of office work that made an automatic writing machine useful. As a general rule, technological inventions followed in the wake of changes in capitalism and in the reorganization of the labor process.

A second characteristic of the reorganization of office work was the growth of hierarchical structures of authority. These tended to replace the idiosyncratic, personal control of owners and managers with codified, impersonal rules. The existence of codified procedures for decision making meant that clerical workers had fewer opportunities to make decisions, and their control over their jobs was consequently diminished. A legion of rules covering all areas of office life accompanied this formalization of office hierarchy—rules about the degree of punctuality required, proper office attire, and what constituted "businesslike" behavior. The point is not that these features of office work were never dictated by employers in the small, pre–1870 office, but that the direct personal control of employers over their clerical employees was being replaced by the impersonal control of hierarchical structures and codified rules.

The elaboration of the division of labor and the creation of hierarchical structures of authority affected low-level clerical workers most directly. But the reorganization also brought into being the private secretary, whose work was typical of higher-level clerical workers.

Unlike the scientifically managed clerical worker, the private secretary was expected to take the initiative in his or her work, which consisted of an almost infinitely wide variety of tasks. The private secretary and the executive for whom he or she worked divided between them all of the duties involved in the latter's job. The governing principle of the division was that the executive's time, attention and energy should be saved for the "important," creative aspects of the task, with the private secretary doing the menial parts. In practice, of course, the division of labor varied a good deal. A private secretary might be restricted to specific tasks because the executive liked to see to all details himself, or a private secretary might do most of the executive's work. In either case, the secretary was the executive's personal servant, with tasks defined by his personal choice.

Private secretaries often used their understanding of office operations to take the initiative in changing them. Their work, then, was an integrated whole, much as office work in general had been prior to 1870. Furthermore, private secretaries were, to some extent, apprentice executives. But their apprenticeship had become permanent. In the late nineteenth and early twentieth centuries, when most private secretaries were men, some had been promoted to executive positions. But this was no longer true by 1930, when women dominated this position. Notwithstanding the various success stories of female executives who had started out as private secretaries, the literature on private secretaries began to warn that the position was by no means a stepping-stone toward management. As gender changed, there was a significant decrease in promotion opportunities. The male private secretary might some day sit in an executive's chair; the female was, as a rule, an office wife or servant whose chances of moving up in the corporate world were virtually nil.

The relationship between an employer and a private secretary remained very personal. The division of labor between them often depended less on codified rules than on the personal characteristics of those involved; that is, on how much initiative a private secretary was interested in taking and how much the employer was willing to assign. The myriad personal services that the private secretary performed, from placing telephone calls to going out to buy sandwiches, underscored the personal nature of their relations.

By 1930, therefore, the reorganization of clerical work had produced two distinct kinds of clerical workers. On the one hand there were low-level clerical workers—file clerks, typists, office machine operators, and so on—who, to use Harry Braverman's terminology, were not expected to participate in the conception of their work. They were to concern themselves only with its execution. This confinement to the routine execution of a relatively small number of tasks diminished their control. They had been deprived of any larger understanding of their jobs and had lost the opportunity to use any initiative. Their work had been severely degraded by comparison with office work before the late nineteenth century.

Private secretaries, on the other hand, had much more independence and control. They were still encouraged to use their initiative in the execution of a wide variety of tasks. By 1930, however, the promotional opportunities that they had once enjoyed to a limited extent had pretty much dried up. Furthermore, they were often asked to work as the personal servants of their executives, and routinely carried out some pretty menial tasks.

It would be hard to overemphasize the importance of the difference between the work of these two basic categories of office workers, especially since people often ascribed what were distinctive attributes of the private secretary's duties to *all* office work. Consequently, all office jobs could be described in glamorous tones as "working as a team with an important executive" and "never having a dull moment in sophisticated surroundings." Thus the drab realities of work in the typing pool or file room could be effectively disguised, at least in the newspaper job listings. Admittedly, low-level clerical workers were promoted. The personal histories of many private secretaries started out with an account of how an executive had noticed and appreciated certain initiatives that "that little typist or stenographer" had taken, and how she had then been hired as his private secretary. Because there were such promotions, all office work was seen as a continuum, with a low-level clerical job being the first step on the occupational ladder. But there were real differences between the two kinds of jobs.

Economic forces, which were responsible for this reorganization of office work, also prompted changes in the work force itself. The feminization of clerical work was simply the result of the exigencies of demand and supply. The rapid expansion of capitalist firms and government agencies, accompanied by the growth of correspondence and record keeping, led to a mounting demand for clerical labor. That demand was met, in part, by the availability of literate female labor. A number of factors contributed to the existence of this labor force. The economic instability of small farm and small business families both released women's labor to the paid labor force and made the income women could earn more important. Clerical work was more desirable than other working-class jobs, both because of the higher wages it offered and the comparatively high status it enjoyed. The decline of productive work in the home also released women's labor to the labor force, and few other jobs specifically requiring literacy were open to women. Furthermore, the supply of literate male labor was being tapped not only for the burgeoning clerical field, but also for management and professional positions, which rapidly increased in number with late nineteenth-century capitalist expansion. These factors, rather than technological innovation, explain the changes in clerical work.

Technological change did, however, facilitate the feminization of clerical work. New office machines, the most prevalent form of technological change, were gender-neutral. Being new, they had not been associated with the male-dominated early nineteenth-century office. Consequently, women hired to operate them were not met by the argument that they were employed at "men's" machines or encroaching upon "men's work." The lack of such protest facilitated their entry into clerical jobs associated with new machines. This in no way suggests, it must be emphasized, that various office machines were more "suited" to female labor than to male. Although many made this claim, notably in the case of the typewriter, the fact that, outside the United States, typists were often men suggests otherwise. It was not because the typewriter was more "suited" to female labor, but because it was gender-neutral that women's entry into the office was facilitated.

Other factors also facilitated the feminization of clerical workers. Perhaps the most important was the reorganized division of labor. Many clerical jobs, relatively integrated prior to 1870, were subjected to a radical division of labor as offices expanded. This resulted in a large number of routine, repetitive, low-level, dead-end clerical tasks, often filled by women. Thus the degradation of clerical work included a shift from one sex to another. Following an office reorganization, a male nineteenth-century bookkeeper would not, in all likelihood, find himself demoted to a low-level job in the bookkeeping department. Instead, he would probably be gracefully retired, or else put in charge of the bookkeeping department, with that department's low-level jobs very likely being filled by women. Since they were not directly competitive with the male bookkeepers, potential opposition to them doing men's work in this department would be muted. Reorganization thus frustrated the possibility of women directly pushing men out of jobs, a development that might have served as a deterrent to feminization.

A third factor that eased women's employment as office workers was their recruitment as clerks in the Treasury Department during the Civil War. This radical wartime "experiment" provided an often cited precedent for hiring women clerical workers that the expanding businesses of the late nineteenth century followed.

Finally, patriarchal social patterns help to explain why women were concentrated in the clerical, as opposed to managerial, positions in the expanding office sector. In a society where men were dominant and women subordinate, it seemed only natural that men occupied the higher-level jobs.

The patterns of patriarchy also affected the extent to which office workers saw themselves as belonging to the "clerical class." By and large, employers and managers were men while clerical workers were women. This was the case with private secretaries by 1930; and even the low-level clerical workers whose immediate supervisors were women were likely to see only men as they looked up the ladder of the office hierarchy. Thus there was a tendency, particularly obvious in the literature on private secretaries, for bosses to be seen as males first and as employers or managers second. Theirs was often perceived as predominantly a male, rather than as a class, authority.

To the extent that female clerical workers hesitated to challenge their male employers and supervisors *because* they were men, the gender-specific character of office hierarchies served to stabilize class relations. Women reared in a male-dominated society and shaped by patterns of male dominance in a variety of ways, both subtle and direct, were trained to submit to male authority. Thus the feminization of clerical labor meant a docile workforce and helped to stabilize the power relations between office workers and management.

The fact that female clerical workers were often identified as women first and as workers second reinforced the assumption, probably shared by many of them, that a woman's primary role in life was to marry and raise a family. Such a perception tended in itself to distract women from their membership in the clerical class. And female office workers who gave primacy to their domestic role were likely to leave the office and the labor force when they married or, at the latest, started having children.

It should not be thought that women, voluntarily or by their "natures," chose to emphasize their gender instead of class identification. This was a question not of choice but of women's structural position in society. Their place in a variety of institutions made women more likely to submit to male authority rather than to challenge it openly. Certainly up until 1930, most families in the United States were dominated by systems of male authority that allowed women little formal power. It was not until 1920 that women even had the right to vote in federal elections. Women did not necessarily choose to submit to male authority; rather, they were both trained to do so from birth and, in many cases, simply denied the right to do anything else. The lack of promotional opportunities and the degrading nature of many of the jobs offer further evidence of the structural, as opposed to voluntary, basis for female clerical workers' identification with their gender rather than with their class. Such conditions tended to push women out of the clerical labor force. A woman who had to choose between a life of domestic work and working at a deadening low-level clerical job or as an executive's personal servant earning no public recognition whatsoever was not given much of a choice. Instead of arguing that women were simply "choosing" to leave the office in order to go home and tend the hearth, it makes more sense to maintain that their structural position in the office as well as in society at large pushed them out of the clerical labor force after a relatively short tenure within it.

Aspects of the organization of clerical work itself also militated against the development of class identity among clerical workers. The relationship between a private secretary and his or her employer was, in some ways, deeply personal. The secretary was in effect a servant, expected to be trustworthy beyond reproach and to carry out many non-business errands for him. Such duties and such a relationship militated against secretaries perceiving their work situation in structural or class terms. They were more likely to assess it in terms of their individual employer, than in terms of the conditions they shared with other private secretaries. Much as in a nineteenth-century office, the behavior of the individual employer loomed large: if he was "nice," considerate, and so on, then the job could be enjoyable or at least not oppressive; if he was a tartar or treated his secretary like a doormat, then the job could be unbearable. That private secretaries were actively encouraged to identify their interests with their employers rather than with other private secretaries also contributed to such a perception. And it could only be enhanced by the fact that private secretaries, working alone in individual offices, were isolated from other members of their class.

Low-level clericals usually did not work in the same degree of isolation. But there were other factors discouraging them from seeing their situation in class terms. First of all, the private secretary and the low-level clerical worker were not always distinguished from each other, a confusion that was probably shared by some low-level clerical workers themselves. Furthermore, the job of private secretary was often considered the ultimate promotional goal of these workers, and one that was by no means unattainable. Consequently, thinking of themselves as future private secretaries, they identified with private secretaries and were thereby discouraged from perceiving their situation in class terms.

Competition among clerical workers, fostered by management, also retarded the development of a common class perception. The institution of bonus and premium plans, the attempts to foster a "spirit of friendly rivalry," and even the creation of finely delineated (and sometimes meaningless) hierarchical levels within clerical work all encouraged clerical workers to compete with one another. Although management often initiated these competitive schemes in order to prod clerical workers to higher levels of productivity, they also had the effect of disguising clerical workers' common class position.

But clerical workers grouped together in large work units had more opportunity to observe their common class interests. Indeed, David Lockwood found that the size of a firm was the best indicator of whether or not a clerk in Britain was likely to join a union—the larger the firm, the more likely the clerk was to be a union member. Clerical workers who worked in the relative isolation of small offices were likely to attribute their situation to the peculiarities of their firm, rather than to their structural position.

We return in the end to the significance of the feminization of the clerical labor force. It meant that the degradation of clerical work and the proletarianization of office workers was disguised. To the extent that female office workers were seen as women first and workers second, the decline in their position relative to their nineteenth-century predecessors' was masked. Instead of the process being seen as proletarianization, the shift merely appeared to be from male to female office workers. Among the many assumptions about women that identified them as women a very strong first and as workers a very weak second was the idea that women were primarily concerned with being or becoming wives, mothers, and housewives. Hence their jobs were considered relatively unimportant to them—a means of filling time and earning a little extra money until marriage. Furthermore, it was often assumed that women, in part because of their past or future familial roles, were meant to be subservient to men. Finally, they were believed uniquely suited to boring, menial tasks where qualities of leadership or independence were totally unnecessary. Such beliefs could become self-fulfilling prophecies. If a woman saw that her future in office work was limited, she might well perceive marriage and domestic life as a welcome alternative. Had office work been more promising, with job possibilities offering challenges and a certain degree of power, she might have been more reluctant to marry or to quit work upon marriage. But such was not the case, and if they had the chance many women left office employment after a few years, thereby lending support to the claim that they cared mainly about being wives, mothers, and housekeepers. The process of degradation that had taken place throughout much of office work from the nineteenth to the twentieth centuries was thereby disguised. The nineteenth-century clerk had not turned into a proletarian; he had merely turned into a woman.

Appendix

Table 1.   Clerical Workers in the United States, by Sex, 1870–1930

Job Category	1870	1880	1890
Bookkeepers, cashiers, and accountants			
Total	38,776	74,919	159,374
Male	37,892*	70,667[†]	131,602
Female	884[:]	4,252[†]	27,772
% Female	2.0	5.7	17.4
Office clerks			
Total	29,801	59,799	187,969
Male	28,878[§]	59,484[†]	163,686[†]
Female	923[i]	315[†]	24,283[†]
% Female	3.1	.5	12.9
Messenger, errand, and office boys/girls			
Total	8,046	12,818	47,183
Male	7,967[#]	12,421	44,294
Female	79	397	2,889
% Female	.9	3.1	6.1
Stenographers and typists			
Total	154	5,000	33,418
Male	147	3,000[†]	12,148
Female	7	2,000[†]	21,270
% Female	4.5	40.0	63.6

SOURCE: Alba M. Edwards, *Comparative Occupation Statistics for the United States, 1870 to 1940*. Part of the Sixteenth Census of the United States: 1940 (Washington, D.C.: Government Printing Office, 1943), Tables 9 and 10.

NOTES

* Census figures estimated, and 372 added because of undercount in thirteen Southern states. For an explanation of the undercount, see Edwards, *Comparative Occupation Statistics*, Appendix A, note 3.

[†] All figures estimated. For information about how estimates were arrived at see Edwards, *Comparative Occupation Statistics*, Appendix A, notes 32, 42, 43 and 44.

1900	1910	1920	1930
254,880	486,700	734,688	930,648
180,727	299,545	375,564	447,937
74,153	187,155	359,124	482,711
29.1	38.5	48.8	51.9
248,323	720,498	1,487,905	1,997,000
229,991[†]	597,833	1,015,742	1,290,447
18,332[†]	122,665	472,163	706,553
7.4	17.0	31.7	35.4
66,009	108,035	113,022	90,379
59,392	96,748	98,768	81,430
6,617	11,287	14,254	8,949
10.0	10.4	12.6	9.9
112,364	316,693	615,154	811,190
26,246	53,378	50,410	36,050
86,118	263,315	564,744	755,140
76.6	83.1	91.8	95.4

[:] Census figures estimated, and 2 added because of undercount in thirteen Southern states.
[§] Census figures estimated, and 488 added because of undercount in thirteen Southern states.
[‖] Census figures estimated, and 6 added because of undercount in thirteen Southern states.
[#] 70 added because of undercount in thirteen Southern states.

Table 2. High School and College Graduates in the United States, 1870–1970.*

Year of Graduation	High School			College		
	Total	Men	Women	Total	Men	Women
1870	16,000	7,064	8,936	9,371	7,591	1,780
1880	23,634	10,605	13,029	10,353	7,868	2,485
1890	43,731	18,549	25,182	14,306	10,157	4,149
1900	94,883	38,075	56,808	25,324	17,220	8,104
1910	156,429	63,676	92,753	34,178	22,557	11,621
1920	311,266	123,684	187,582	48,622	31,980	16,642
1930	666,904	300,376	366,528	122,484	73,615	48,869
1940	1,221,475	578,718	642,757	186,500	109,546	76,954
1950	1,199,700	570,700	629,000	432,058	328,841	103,217
1960	1,864,000	898,000	966,000	392,000	254,000	138,000
1970	2,906,000	1,439,000	1,467,000	827,000	484,000	343,000

SOURCE: Federal Security Agency, Office of Education, *Biennial Survey of Education.* Cited in *Statistical Abstract of the United States*, 1952 (p. 121) and 1972 (p. 127).

NOTE: *Table 2 compares the numbers of male and female high school and college graduates, 1870–1970. The data cover graduates of both public and private institutions.

Table 3. Farmers, Business Owners and Managers, and
Professionals, 1870–1930

Year	Farmers	% of Labor Force	Business Owners and Managers	% of Labor Force	Professionals	% of Labor Force
1870	3,127,715	24.2	535,012	4.1	377,197	2.9
1880	4,301,412	24.7	746,136	4.3	596,097	3.4
1890	5,382,037	23.1	1,134,617	4.9	929,934	4.0
1900	5,772,610	19.9	1,408,446	4.8	1,215,109	4.2
1910	6,182,676	16.5	2,048,089	5.5	1,752,366	4.7
1920	6,479,684	15.3	2,364,718	5.6	2,220,399	5.2
1930	6,079,234	12.4	3,212,674	6.6	3,176,929	6.5

SOURCE: Alba M. Edwards, *Comparative Occupation Statistics for the United States, 1870 to 1940*. Part of the Sixteenth Census of the United States: 1940 (Washington: Government Printing Office, 1943). Tables 9 and 10, pp. 113–129.

Table 4. Women in Selected Occupations, 1870–1930

Job Category	1870		1880		1890	
	No.	As % of total employed in occupation	No.	As % of total employed in occupation	No.	As % of total employed in occupation
Clerical workers*	1,910	2.3	7,040	4.4	77,060	16.4
Teachers'	84,548	65.9	153,372	67.8	244,467	70.9
Trained nurses	1,154	95.8	1,464	95.2	4,206	91.8
Social, welfare, and religious workers:	68	0.1	165	0.3	1,143	1.3
Artists, sculptors, and teachers of art	414	10.0	2,061	22.6	10,815	48.1
Musicians and teachers of music	5,806	35.9	13,182	43.2	34,519	55.5
Lawyers, judges, and justices; abstracters, notaries, and justices of the peace	5	0.0	75	0.1	208	0.2

SOURCE: Alba M. Edwards, *Comparative Occupational Statistics for the United States, 1870 to 1940*; Part of the Sixteenth Census of the United States: 1940 (Washington: Government Printing Office, 1943).

* Includes agents, collectors, and credit men; bookkeepers, cashiers, and accountants; clerks (except clerks in stores); messenger, errand and office boys and girls; stenographers and typists.
' Includes college presidents and professors for 1870–1900, although given the data for subsequent years, it is unlikely that they ever amounted to more than 2% of the total.
: Includes clergymen for 1870–1900.

1900		1910		1920		1930	
No.	As % of total employed in occupation	No.	As % of total employed in occupation	No.	As % of total employed in occupation	No.	As % of total employed in occupation
7,053	25.4	588,609	34.2	1,421,925	45.7	1,986,830	49.4
5,485	73.5	478,027	79.8	639,241	83.9	860,278	81.0
1,046	93.6	76,508	92.9	143,664	96.3	288,737	98.1
3,373	3.0	8,889	55.7	26,927	65.5	44,543	71.2
1,021	44.3	15,429	45.2	14,617	41.3	21,644	37.8
2,359	56.8	84,478	60.6	72,678	55.8	79,611	48.2
1,010	0.9	1,343	1.1	3,221	2.6	5,293	3.1

Table 5.　Civil Service Examinations, 1 January to 1 July 1919, by Sex

Service	No. of occupations for which examinations were held	Open to men and women	Open to women only	Open to men only	% closed to wome
Biological science service	52	18	2	32	61.5
Physical science service	31	11	—	20	64.5
Medical science service	16	3	1	12	75.0
Engineering service	40	13	—	27	67.5
Economic and sociological service	7	—	—	7	100.0
Miscellaneous professional service (editorial work, teaching, nursing)	10	5	2	3	30.0
Managerial and other expert office service	8	6	—	2	25.0
Clerical service	44	37	—	7	15.9
Mechanical and manufacturing service	46	5	1	40	87.0
Domestic, reformatory and rural service	6	—	1	5	83.3
TOTAL	260	98	7	155	59.6

SOURCE: Bertha M. Nienburg, *Women in the Government Service*, U.S. Department of Labor, Women's Bureau, Bulletin no. 8 (Washington: Government Printing Office, 1920), p. 11.

Notes

Chapter 2.

1. Herman Melville, "Bartleby," in *Billy Budd and the Piazza Tales* (Garden City, N.Y.: Doubleday and Co., 1961), pp. 116–21. "Bartleby" was published as one of the *Piazza Tales* in 1856. The lawyer soon added a fourth member to his staff, Bartleby.

2. In 1800 only 322,371 people were classified by the census as urban; there were only 6 cities with a population of more than 10,000, and the single largest city was in the 50,000 to 100,000 range. By contrast, there were 4,986,112 people classified as rural, over fifteen times as many. By 1860 the number of cities had increased: there were 95 cities with a population of more than 10,000 and 9 whose population exceeded 100,000. The 25,226,803 people classified as rural were now only four times the urban population, which stood at 6,216,518. Another index of the agrarian nature of the United States prior to the Civil War is that in 1820 roughly 75 percent of all those gainfully employed worked on farms. Source: Bureau of the Census, U.S. Department of Commerce, *Historical Statistics of the United States: Colonial Times to 1957* (Washington, D.C.: Government Printing Office, 1960), Series A181-194 "Number of Places in Urban and Rural Territory, by Size of Place: 1790–1950," Series A195-209 "Population in Urban and Rural Territory, by Size of Place: 1790–1950," and Series D36-45 "Gainful Workers, by Age, Sex, and Farm-Nonfarm Occupations: 1820 to 1930."

3. Douglass C. North, *The Economic Growth of the United States, 1790–1860* (Englewood Cliffs, N.J.: Prentice-Hall, 1961), p. 50.

4. See Gerald C. Fischer, *American Banking Structure* (New York: Columbia University Press, 1968), pp. 9–18; and Harry D. Hutchin-

185

son, *Money, Banking, and the United States Economy* (Englewood Cliffs, N.J.: Prentice-Hall, 1975), pp. 59–61.

5. There is an extensive literature about early New England textile manufacture, particularly about the mills in Lowell, Massachusetts. Two books that focus on the development of the factory system, and on the capitalists who controlled it, are Caroline Ware, *The Early New England Cotton Manufacture: A Study in Industrial Beginnings* (New York: Russell and Russell, 1966 [1931]) and Hannah Josephson, *The Golden Threads: New England's Mill Girls and Magnates* (New York: Duell, Sloane and Pearce, 1949).

6. Melville, "Bartleby," p. 123.

7. William T. Baxter, *The House of Hancock: Business in Boston, 1724–1775* (New York: Russell and Russell, 1965), pp. 195–96.

8. Ibid., p. 197.

9. Stuart Weems Bruchey, *Robert Oliver, Merchant of Baltimore, 1783–1819* (Baltimore: Johns Hopkins Press, 1956), p. 131.

10. Baxter, *The House of Hancock*, p. 146.

11. An extremely detailed history of accounting may be found in Richard Brown, *A History of Accounting and Accountants* (Edinburgh: T. C. and E. C. Jack, 1905). Those interested in accounting in Britain might consult David Murray, *Chapters in the History of Bookkeeping, Accountancy and Commercial Arithmetic* (Glasgow: Jackson, Wylie and Co., 1930), and Nicholas A. H. Stacey, *English Accountancy: A Study in Social and Economic History, 1800–1954* (London: Gee and Co., 1954). Also see Sidney Pollard, *The Genesis of Modern Management: A Study of the Industrial Revolution in Great Britain* (Middlesex, Eng. and Baltimore: Penguin Books, 1965).

12. Baxter, *The House of Hancock*, pp. 17–21 and 35–38.

13. Matthew Josephson, *The Robber Barons: The Great American Capitalists, 1861–1901* (New York: Harcourt, Brace and World, 1934), p. 71.

14. Ibid., p. 18.

15. Henrietta M. Larson, *Jay Cooke, Private Banker* (Cambridge, Mass.: Harvard University Press, 1936), p. 14.

16. Theodore Dreiser, *The Financier* (New York: Harper and Bros., 1912), pp. 48–49.

17. Larson, *Jay Cooke, Private Banker*, p. 19.

18. Ibid., p. 36.

19. "Familiar Scenes in the Life of a Clerk," Part 2, *Hunt's Merchants' Magazine* 6 (1842): 58.

20. William Earl Dodge, "A Great Merchants' Recollections of Old New York, 1818–1880," *Valentine's Manual of Old New York*, no. 5. n.s. (1921): 151. Before the Civil War, the term "clerk" referred to clerks in stores as well as clerks in offices unconnected to stores. Store clerks no doubt waited on customers, but they were also probably expected to do a certain amount of office work.

21. Larson, *Jay Cooke, Private Banker*, p. 38.

22. Alfred Chandler, whose concern is more with managers than with clerical workers, has described the managerial structures of this period. Even in the largest firms, the managerial systems were very rudimentary and direct. A "general superintendent" might be in charge of supervising the workforce, while the president or treasurer would arrange for financing and take care of other financial transactions. "Merchants, manufacturers or railroad officers spent nearly all their time carrying on functional activities. . . . Only occasionally were they obliged to consider long-term plans such as the adoption of new machinery, taking on another line of merchandise, or the finding of a new partner or agent." Alfred D. Chandler, Jr., *Strategy and Structure: Chapters in the History of the Industrial Enterprise* (Cambridge, Mass.: M.I.T. Press, 1962), p. 19.

23. "At length the hour of shutting up the counting-house arrived [on Christmas Eve]. With an ill-will Scrooge dismounted from his stool, and tacitly admitted the fact to the expectant clerk in the Tank, who instantly snuffed his candle out, and put on his hat.

"'You'll want all day to-morrow, I suppose?' said Scrooge.

"'If quite convenient, sir.'

"'It's not convenient,' said Scrooge, 'and it's not fair. If I was to stop half-a-crown for it, you'd think yourself ill used, I'll be bound?'

"The clerk smiled faintly.

"'And yet,' said Scrooge, 'you don't think *me* ill used, when I pay a day's wages for no work.'

"The clerk observed that it was only once a year.

"'A poor excuse for picking a man's pocket every twenty-fifth of December!' said Scrooge, buttoning his great-coat to the chin. 'But I suppose you must have the whole day. Be here all the earlier the next morning!'"

Charles Dickens, *A Christmas Carol* (Baltimore: Penguin Books, 1971 [1843]), p. 53.

24. "Familiar Scenes in the Life of a Clerk," *Hunt's Merchants' Magazine* 5 (1841): 536.

25. Josephson, *The Robber Barons*, p. 38. The moral of this story is not clear. Crime does or does not pay, depending on how you look at it.

26. "Familiar Scenes in the Life of a Clerk," Part 2, p. 56.

27. William T. Baxter, *Daniel Henchman: A Colonial Bookseller* (Salem, Mass.: Essex Institute, 1934), p. 2.

28. Baxter, *The House of Hancock*, pp. 147–48.

29. Ibid., p. 199.

30. "Familiar Scenes in the Life of a Clerk," p. 536.

31. Charles Booth, "Population Classified by Trades," *Life and Labour of the People in London*, vol. 7 (1896), pp. 278–79. Cited in David Lockwood, *The Blackcoated Worker: A Study in Class Consciousness* (London: Unwin University Books, 1958), p. 32.

32. Baxter, *The House of Hancock*, pp. 146–47.

33. "Familiar Scenes in the Life of a Clerk," p. 540.

34. David Lockwood describes a similar situation in English countinghouses, where relatively high-born men worked as clerks to learn the business alongside more lowly born clerks who had little chance of advancement. The clerks who were in fact apprentice merchants even worked for reduced wages in return for the opportunity of learning the trade, a situation that did the wages of the men who would always be clerks no good.

"'There is a wide distinction,' says one commentator, 'between the clerk by profession and the clerk in *statu pupillari*. The merchant, the banker, the solicitor, and the novice in almost any trade or profession, begins to learn his duty as a clerk—it is the only way in which he is initiated; in his case it is only a state of preparation, not even of probation; his station in life, his actual capital, or his influential connections, give him a *locus standi* before he is qualified to fill it; to enable him to fill it with credit and advantage, he must learn the elements of business; and therefore he is placed as a clerk at the desk, but only temporarily, till he can undertake the management of the same business in its higher departments (*The Clerk: A Sketch in Outline of His Duties and Discipline*, Houlston's Industrial Library No. 7 [London: 1878], p. 49). . . .'

"Out of a total of 1,370 clerks employed by some 350 firms, only

420 were salaried clerks, while no less than 950 were apprentices, that is to say, 'usually lads of good family, and well supplied with pocket money, to whom, by virtue of their scanty pay, special facilities for learning the business are extended to the exclusion and disadvantage of the smaller body.'" Lockwood, *The Blackcoated Worker*, pp. 25–26.

35. Baxter, *The House of Hancock*, p. 421.

36. Dodge, "A Great Merchant's Recollections of Old New York, 1818–1880," p. 173.

37. Larson, *Jay Cooke, Private Banker*, p. 56.

38. Stephan Thernstrom, *Poverty and Progress: Social Mobility in a Nineteenth Century City* (Cambridge, Mass.: Harvard University Press, 1964), p. 145.

39. Oscar Handlin, *Boston's Immigrants, 1790–1880* (New York: Atheneum, 1970 [1941]), pp. 67–68.

40. Harry Braverman, *Labor and Monopoly Capital: The Degradation of Work in the Twentieth Century* (New York and London: Monthly Review Press, 1974), p. 293.

41. Lockwood, *The Blackcoated Worker*, p. 33.

Chapter 3.

1. Harry Braverman, *Labor and Monopoly Capital: The Degradation of Work in the Twentieth Century* (New York and London: Monthly Review Press, 1974), pp. 302–3.

2. It is difficult to find precise information about exactly what changes were made in office organization as the number of clerical workers grew from five, say, to forty-five. In general, the writers of business histories have been much more interested in issues such as how a company amassed the capital to open a new plant or buy out a competitor than in questions of the organization of clerical work, a subject that is sometimes referred to as a "reorganization of the staff" without further elaboration.

One point, however, can be made with relative certainty: the development of office organization during this period was extremely uneven, varying a great deal from firm to firm. First of all, despite the rapid expansion and consolidation of capitalist firms at the end of the nineteenth century, petit capitalist businesses by no means entirely disappeared. So while the large corporations might be forced into a "reorganization of the staff" because of their rapid growth, other firms that somehow managed to survive without growing all that much could continue office procedures that dated back to before the Civil War. Even among the large corporations, there was great variation in the extent and form of office reorganizations. For example, it was in the 1850s that Daniel C. McCallum made some of the first innovations in administrative restructuring for the Erie Railroad. And, according to Alfred Chandler, by the end of World War I, "most large industrial companies whose executives paid any attention to organizational matters were administered through much the same type of organization—the centralized, functionally departmentalized structure: (Alfred D. Chandler, Jr., *Strategy and Structure: Chapters in the History of the Industrial Enterprise* [Cambridge, Mass.: M.I.T. Press, 1962], p. 40). However, there were some large corporations that were very late to reorganize the administrative part of their operations. The most notorious example was Henry Ford, who refused to remove his finger from any of the auto company's numerous pies and insisted on having a large majority of decisions about everything from the acquisition of raw materials to the sale of the automobiles go across his desk. Ford hung onto these anachronistic management practices into the 1930s and 1940s; bankruptcy was narrowly averted only by the advent of Henry Ford II, who introduced "modern management" practices.

3. Chandler, *Strategy and Structure*, p. 2.

4. Ibid., pp. 21–22.

5. There was an earlier method for copying letters and documents in which a sheet of damp tissue paper was pressed against the original, rendering a legible copy. Carbon paper was in limited use in the early nineteenth century, but it was only after the introduction of the typewriter with its hard-hitting keys that its use became widespread. By the 1880s stencil duplicating machines were in use, but it was not until the early 1900s that a rotary duplicating machine capable of making many copies relatively quickly was perfected. As early as 1853, William Burroughs had invented an adding machine, but it was not mass-produced and widely distributed until around 1900. And in 1889 Herman Hollerith took out a patent on the machine that is widely regarded as the first practical computer. Hollerith had worked on the U.S. Census of 1880: the laborious tabulation by hand of

so many numbers made the usefulness of a mechanical method for tabulation self-evident. Hollerith's computer was used in the 1890 census, and Hollerith himself went on to start the company that became International Business Machines (IBM) in 1924. A myriad of other office machines, such as the postal meter and the automatic envelope-addressing machine, were invented and put into use in the last years of the nineteenth and the first years of the twentieth centuries.

For more information on the history of office machines, see the chapter entitled "Abacus to Pocket Calculator" in Alan Delgado, *The Enormous File: A Social History of the Office* (London: John Murray, 1979); W. B. Proudfoot, *The Origin of Stencil Duplicating* (London: Hutchinson, 1972); Herman H. Goldstine, *The Computer from Pascal to von Neumann* (Princeton: Princeton University Press, 1972); and Alfred D. Chandler, Jr., *The Visible Hand: The Managerial Revolution in American Business* (Cambridge, Mass.: Harvard University Press, 1977).

6. My account of the development of the typewriter is based primarily on two sources: Richard N. Current, *The Typewriter and the Men Who Made It* (Urbana: University of Illinois Press, 1954); and Bruce Bliven, Jr., *The Wonderful Writing Machine* (New York: Random House, 1954).

7. Bliven, *The Wonderful Writing Machine*, p. 30.

8. Cited in ibid., pp. 30–31.

9. Ibid., p. 42.

10. Cited in Current, *The Typewriter*, p. 28.

11. Ibid., pp. 48–49.

12. Ibid., p. 64.

13. Cited in Bliven, *The Wonderful Writing Machine*, p. 61.

14. Ibid.

15. Ibid., p. 62.

16. Current, *The Typewriter*, p. 117.

17. Cited in Bliven, *The Wonderful Writing Machine*, pp. 70–71.

18. Cited in Current, *The Typewriter*, p. 110.

19. See Richard C. Edwards, "Alienation and Inequality: Capitalist Relations of Production in Bureaucratic Enterprises" (Ph.D. diss., Harvard University, 1972). Edwards also discusses the system of "structural control," where the very manner in which workers perform their assigned tasks is defined by the capitalist or manager. The

corporation, according to Edwards, has imposed "structural control over work activities. The organization, coordination, and assignment of work tasks is embedded in a larger structure of work. The Pace of work, along with specific direction in how the work tasks are to be completed, is determined by this structure. The Structure, being both more comprehensive than the immediate workplace of foremen and workers and having been imposed from a higher level, removes from the foreman's hands the initiative control over the flow of work. The foreman's role in the production process is transformed to one of merely enforcing an already pre-structured flow of work activities. Power was thus made invisible in the structure of work, rather than exercised openly by the foreman or supervisor" (pp. 99–100).

This phenomenon will be taken up at length in the chapter on scientific management in the office.

20. This account of N. W. Ayer and Son is based on Ralph M. Hower, *The History of an Advertising Agency: N. W. Ayer and Son at Work, 1869–1939* (Cambridge, Mass.: Harvard University Press, 1939). Even though Hower's book sheds more light on office procedures than do most other business histories, it still focuses on office managers and owners rather than mere clerical workers, so that some of the information about clerical work at Ayer's must be found between the lines.

21. It is interesting to note that even though Ayer's seems to have been rather ahead of itself in bureaucratic organization and reorganization, it still engaged in a rather outmoded practice—the acceptance of goods in kind (books, patent medicine) as payment for services rendered. This practice was not to last long, however. Hower notes that "by 1890 the agency had given up accepting merchandise in settlement of accounts with advertisers." Ibid., p. 491.

22. Ibid., p. 496.

23. Ibid., pp. 496–97.

24. Ibid., p. 497.

25. Cited in ibid., p. 507. My emphasis.

26. Cited in ibid., p. 521. My emphasis.

27. Ibid., p. 567.

28. Ibid., pp. 540–41. My emphasis.

29. Cited in ibid., pp. 543–44.

30. Ibid., pp. 544–45. Emphasis in the original.

31. Ibid., pp. 561–62.

32. Ibid., p. 532.

33. Cited in ibid., p. 533. Emphasis in the original.

34. And "in 1899 the Ayer management inaugurated a policy of hiring a few college graduates from time to time in order to improve its personnel. The first person so chosen was a Dartmouth man of the class of 1899." Ibid., p. 534. Gone is the policy of having future executives start out as office boys.

35. Ibid., p. 563. My emphasis.

36. Ibid., p. 536.

Chapter 4.

1. "Women in Business: I," *Fortune*, 12, no. 1 (July 1935): 53.

2. "Female Government Clerks in America," *Chambers's Journal* 65 (14 January 1888): 29.

3. "Women in Business: I," p. 53.

4. "Female Government Clerks in America," p. 29.

5. Cindy S. Aron, "'To Barter Their Souls for Gold': Female Clerks in Federal Government Offices, 1862–1890," *Journal of American History* 67 (March 1981): 843.

6. Helen L. Sumner, *History of Women in Industry in the United States*, Volume 9 of the *Report on Condition of Woman and Child Wage-Earners in the United States*, U.S. Senate document no. 645 (Washington, D.C.: Government Printing Office, 1910), pp. 238–40.

7. Ralph M. Hower, *The History of an Advertising Agency: N. W. Ayer and Son at Work, 1869–1939* (Cambridge, Mass.: Harvard University Press, 1939), pp. 535–36.

8. When typewriters were first being marketed, the person who operated one was also called a "typewriter." This confusion of terminology left the door wide open to a whole series of bad jokes, such as this one retold by Bruce Bliven: "the story about the young businessman who had suffered a sudden reverse and wrote to his wife: 'Dear Blanche: I have sold off all my office furniture, chairs, desks, etc., etc., and I am writing this letter under difficulties with my typewriter on my lap.'" (Bruce Bliven, Jr., *The Wonderful Writing Machine* (New York: Random House, 1954), pp. 72–73. I will use the term "typist" throughout to refer to the person who operated a typewriter. This should eliminate any confusion.

9. Bliven, *The Wonderful Writing Machine*, p. 60.

10. Cited in Richard N. Current, *The Typewriter and the Men Who Made It* (Urbana: University of Illinois Press, 1954), p. 86.

11. U.S. Department of Labor, Women's Bureau, *The Effects of Applied Research upon the Employment Opportunities of American Women* (Washington: Government Printing Office, n.d.), p. 42. My emphasis.

12. Bliven, *The Wonderful Writing Machine*, pp. 71–72.

13. For further discussion of this point, see Heidi Hartmann, "The Unhappy Marriage of Marxism and Feminism: Towards a More Progressive Union," in Lydia Sargent, ed., *Women and Revolution: A Discussion of the Unhappy Marriage of Marxism and Feminism* (Boston, Mass.: South End Press, 1981).

14. Figures compiled from Table 4, "Number of Persons Engaged in Specified Occupations, for Both Sexes and for Each Sex Separately: 1870, 1880, 1890, and 1900," in the introductory chapter on the "Comparison at Twelfth and Preceding Censuses"; Bureau of the Census, Department of Commerce and Labor, Special Report of the 12th Census: *Occupations at the 12th Census* (Washington D.C.: Government Printing Office, 1904), p. 1.

15. Figures cited in C. Wright Mills, *White Collar: The American Middle Classes* (New York: Oxford University Press, 1951), p. 16.

16. See Appendix, Table 5. It should be remembered, however, that the census data on which this table is based do not distinguish between large and small capitalists, although it is safe to assume that the number of truly large capitalists was never very great. Furthermore, the census data consistently lump together proprietors and managers of various kinds of companies. Despite the fact that the twentieth century witnessed the transformation of many an entrepreneur into a salaried manager, these new managers probably had much in common with small businessmen. Their precise relationship to the ownership of production had changed, it is true, but less quantifiable factors such as their sense of class identity and patterns of consumption probably did not differ all that much from those of the classic petite bourgeoisie.

17. C. Wright Mills notes that "in the four decades prior to World War II, the number of firms in existence rose from 1 to 2 million, but during the same period nearly 16 million firms began operation, and at least 14 million went out of business." *White Collar*, p. 23.

18. Ibid., p. 31.

19. Booth Tarkington, *Alice Adams* (Garden City, N.Y.: Doubleday, Page and Co., 1921), pp. 433–34.

20. Aron, "'To Barter Their Souls for Gold,'" p. 841.

21. Grace L. Coyle, "Women in the Clerical Occupations," *Annals of the American Academy of Political and Social Science* 143 (May 1929): 182–83.

22. "Average Weekly Earnings during Whole Time Employed for Selected Female Workers: Boston, 1883," in *15th Annual Report of the Massachusetts Bureau of Statistics of Labor*, Part I: "The Working Girls of Boston" (Boston: Wright and Potter, 1884).

23. "Average Net Income of Women Workers in Boston, by Occupation: 1910," in Louise Marion Bosworth, *The Living Wage of Women Workers: A Study of Incomes and Expenditures of 450 Women in the City of Boston* (New York: Longmans, Green, and Co., 1911), p. 16.

24. Coyle, "Women in the Clerical Occupations," p. 181.

25. What remains of that correspondence, consisting mainly of letters from Maimie to Mrs. Howe (as they always referred to each other), is in the archives of the Arthur and Elizabeth Schlesinger Library on the History of Women in America at Radcliffe College in Cambridge, Massachusetts. The letters have also been reprinted in Ruth Rosen and Sue Davidson, eds., *The Maimie Papers* (Old Westbury, N.Y.: Feminist Press, 1977).

26. Maimie Pomerantz Jacobs, Papers, 1910–1922, Schlesinger Library.

27. Miriam Finn Scott, "Sarah and Mr. Salamovitch," *Outlook* 87 (1907): 531.

28. Ibid., pp. 533–34.

29. Ibid., pp. 536–37.

30. Dorothy Richardson, *The Long Day: The Story of a New York Working Girl* (1905). Reprinted in William L. O'Neill, ed., *Women at Work* (Chicago: Quadrangle Books, 1972), p. 271.

31. One of the best accounts I know of productive work in the home is the series of books written by Laura Ingalls Wilder about growing up in a homesteading family in the western United States during the last three decades of the nineteenth century. From the *Little House in the Big Woods* of Wisconsin to the *Little House on the Prairie* of the Dakota Territories, these books contain a myriad of de-

tails about the home life of the Ingalls family. The reduction in the amount of work done in the home is reflected in the books, as the family moves from situations of pure homesteading, with the nearest neighbors two miles away, to life in western towns, where more goods are available in stores and less produced in the home. Although these are children's books, I would recommend them to anyone interested in a first-hand account of life in the United States in the late nineteenth century.

32. Gerda Lerner, "The Lady and the Mill Girl: Changes in the Status of Women in the Age of Jackson," *Mid-Continent American Studies Journal* 10 (Spring 1969).

33. Tarkington, *Alice Adams*, p. 27.

34. For an interesting account of the class origins of nurses, their changing class status, and the growth of division of labor and hierarchical stratification in United States hospitals, see Susan Reverby, "The Emergence of Hospital Nursing," *Health Policy Advisory Center Bulletin* 66 (September–October 1975). Until the 1920s, hospital nursing was done almost entirely by untrained working-class women and unpaid student nurses. In fact, Reverby writes, as late as 1928, "the public often viewed the hospital nursing school as '. . . a sort of respectable reform school where its mental or disciplinary cases can be sent'" (pp. 9–10). Graduate nurses by and large went into private nursing and did not start to stay in hospitals in large numbers until the 1920s and 1930s.

35. Elizabeth Baker, *Technology and Woman's Work* (New York and London: Columbia University Press, 1964), p. 282.

36. J. D. Beveridge, "Efficiency in the Business Department of the High School," *National Education Association Proceedings* (Washington, D.C.: National Education Association: 1912), p. 1039.

37. Janice Harriet Weiss, "Educating for Clerical Work: A History of Commercial Education in the United States since 1850" (Ed.D. diss., Harvard Graduate School of Education, 1978), pp. 37–38. Weiss provides an excellent analytic history of commercial education, both in private business schools and in public high schools.

38. Ibid., p. 77. In 1914–15 there were 208,605 students in public high school commercial courses and 183,286 in private commercial schools.

39. Ibid., p. 174. In 1900, 58.4 percent of all public high school

students, grades nine to twelve, were female; in 1930, 52.0 percent were.

40. Ibid., p. 257.

41. *15th Annual Report of the Massachusetts Bureau of Statistics of Labor*, Part I: "The Working Girls of Boston," Table 1 (Boston: Wright and Potter, 1884).

42. Bureau of the Census, Department of Commerce and Labor, Special Report of the 12th Census (1900), *Statistics of Women at Work* (Washington D.C.: Government Printing Office, 1907), Table 28. The totals of clerical workers of the various races and nativities do not always add up to 100 percent. This discrepancy is contained without explanation in the 1900 Census figures.

43. Ibid., tables 14 and 15.

44. Ibid., table 28.

45. Ibid., table 26.

46. Ibid., table 29.

47. Ibid., table 27.

48. Ibid., tables 26 and 28.

49. Elizabeth Sears, "Business Women and Women in Business," *Harper's Monthly Magazine* 134 (January 1917): 276.

50. Ibid., p. 274.

51. Ibid., pp. 274–75.

Chapter 5.

1. Reproductions of this engraving can be found in Bruce Bliven, Jr., *The Wonderful Writing Machine* (New York: Random House, 1954), p. 73, and in Margery Davies, "Woman's Place Is at the Typewriter: The Feminization of the Clerical Labor Force," *Radical America* 8, no. 4 (July–August 1974): 12.

2. This and all other quotations from this article come from Marion Harland, "The Incapacity of Business Women," *North American Review* 149 (1889): 707–12. The term "business woman" was often applied to any woman employed in a business office, whether she had a clerical or a managerial position.

3. Clara Lanza, "Women Clerks in New York," *Cosmopolitan* 10 (1891): 487–92.

4. Theodora Wadsworth Baker, "Business Woman," *Harper's Weekly* 47 (1903): 1015.

5. Henry Norman, "The Feminine Failure in Business," *Forum* 63 (1920): 455.

6. "Have You a Little 'Deception' Clerk in Your Business?" *Literary Digest* 64 (6 March 1920): 131.

7. R. LeClerc Phillips, "The Temperamental Typist," *North American Review* 227 (1929): 11.

8. Annie Merrill, "Woman in Business," *Canadian Magazine* 21 (1903): 409–10.

9. Harriet Brunkhurst, "The Married Woman in Business," *Collier's, The National Weekly* 44 (26 February 1910): 20.

10. Gissing, an English novelist, provides a particularly interesting, and relatively early, example of this support for the woman office worker. Obviously, in the late nineteenth century England and the United States had different cultures, but the existence of a strong feminist movement in both nations, coupled with the fact that women were entering offices in each, leads one to conclude that Gissing's ideas must have found some resonance on this side of the Atlantic. George Gissing, *The Odd Women* (New York: W. W. Norton and Co., 1971 [1893]).

11. Ibid., p. 54.

12. Ibid., pp. 135–36.

13. Clarence Budington Kelland, "His Wife's Place," *Everybody's Magazine* 41 (November 1919): 17.

14. Ibid., p. 114.

15. Ibid.

16. Norman, "The Feminine Failure in Business," p. 459.

17. Stanley Frost, "What Speed is Worth," *Collier's, The National Weekly* 68 (22 October 1921): 26.

18. Phillips, "The Temperamental Typist," p. 12.

19. Jacques Boyer, "Are Men Better Typists than Women?: Interesting Scientific Tests Made by J. M. Lahy," *Scientific American* 109 (1913): 327.

20. C. E. Smith, letter to the editor in response to "Are Men Better Typists than Women?" *Scientific American* 109 (1913): 411.

21. Ibid.

22. Eleanor Whiting, "Business or the Home for Women?" *Living Age* 217 (1898): 484.

23. By a Successful Business Woman, "Why I Will Not Let My Daughter Go into Business," *Ladies Home Journal* (September 1909): 16.

24. Ibid.

25. Ibid.

26. Gissing, *The Odd Women*, p. 135.

27. Harriet Brunkhurst, "The Home Trials of Business Girls: How Some Mothers Add Unconsciously to Their Daughters' Burdens," *Ladies Home Journal* 27 (September 1910): 30.

28. It does not strike me as accidental that Gissing's heroines were feminists and therefore more likely to question conventional assumptions about woman's place. Harriet Brunkhurst, of all the participants in the debate, seems to have been the most clear-headed about the fact that most women worked in offices out of necessity and were not always in a position to choose marriage.

29. Even leaving aside the strong cultural and psychological forces pushing women to assume that their place really was in the home, it is not hard to see how this assumption, and the accompanying restriction of women to low-level clerical jobs, could easily become a self-fulfilling prophecy. A woman who recognized that her chances of substantial promotion within the office bureaucracy were nil might well decide that it would be rational for her to find a husband to support her. Why should she work at a series of uninteresting routine jobs, to be rewarded only with a moderate income and a gold pin for devoted service when she retired? Having seen the futility of a "Career in Business," she might well decide that the sooner she married and had a family, the better.

30. C. S. Yoakum and Marion A. Bills, "Tests for Office Occupations," *Annals of the American Academy of Political and Social Science* 110 (November 1923): 64.

31. R. C. Schumann, "A Well-Rounded Group of Office Methods," *System* 47 (1925): 738–39.

Chapter 6.

1. Harry Braverman considers scientific management, or Taylorism as it is often called, to be of central importance in the degradation of work under capitalism: "If Taylorism does not exist as a separate

school today, that is because, apart from the bad odor of the name, it is no longer the property of a faction, since its fundamental teachings have become the bedrock of all work design." Harry Braverman, *Labor and Monopoly Capital: The Degradation of Work in the Twentieth Century* (New York and London: Monthly Review Press, 1974), p. 87.

2. "The High Cost of Stenographic Service," *System* 24 (September 1913), advertising section (no page numbers).

3. "The Better Way to Conduct an Office," *World's Work* 10 (1905): 6677–78.

4. Ibid., p. 6677.

5. Ibid., pp. 6678–79.

6. Ibid., p. 6679.

7. Edward D. Page, "The New Science of Business: Making an Office Efficient," *World's Work* 12 (1906): 7683–84. My emphasis.

8. S. A. Peck, "Putting Office Work on a Production Basis: Routing and Control in Office Administration," *Industrial Management* 64 (1922): 358. My emphasis. The struggle over who controlled the work process lasted a long time (1922 was surely not the end of it), in part because clerical workers fought to maintain control, and in part because changes in the size of offices and in their organization did not take place at the same rate everywhere. The reorganization of office production might become necessary relatively early on in one office, while another office might not undergo rapid expansion until twenty or thirty years later.

9. W. H. Leffingwell, "9 Ways to Cut Office Expenses," *System* 41 (1922): 277.

10. Edward Earle Purinton, "Office Efficiency," *Independent* 85 (21 February 1916): 280–81.

11. Chester C. Kaskell, "An Army Plan in Our Offices," *System* 38 (1920): 425.

12. David Lockwood, *The Blackcoated Worker: A Study in Class Consciousness* (London: Unwin University Books, 1958), pp. 92–93.

13. In 1923, for example, the office manager for Graton and Knight Manufacturing Co., tanners and manufacturers of leather belting at Worcester, Massachusetts, wrote that "concerns having exceptionally large office forces, especially those who have a large number of workers on one job or class of work, have been successful in establishing office standardization, as well as piece work or premium systems.

The executives in charge of smaller office forces—say two hundred or under—rightfully feel that their problem is very different, and quite difficult, on account of the variety of work that any one clerk may do. This article will describe the standardization, and establishment of a premium system, in one of these smaller types of office organizations, and will include the description of this system in an accounts receivable department of seven clerks; a voucher record department of one clerk; a Hollerith accounting department of four clerks; a stenographic department of ten clerks; and an order and invoice department of ten clerks." F. E. Barth, "The Premium System in Office Departments: Putting Clerical Work on a Production Basis," *Industrial Management* 65 (1923): 49.

And advice on "saving time in office routine" from an elementary school principal in Seattle, Washington, indicated a familiarity with the principle of scientific management that counseled against having a higher-paid worker do jobs that a lower-paid worker could do: "Many principals do work that the janitor, teachers or pupils should do. When the principal has decided who should do certain work, he should act on his decision. When the principal has determined that he should do a piece of work, that work should be reduced to the best possible routine." While this principal could not have had a very elaborate division of labor in an office that consisted of himself and a clerk, it was clear that he was aware of the ideas in the scientific office management movement and was attempting to apply them to his own situation. Edgar A. Stanton, "Saving Time in Office Routine," *Elementary School Journal* 28 (December 1927): 265.

14. Grace L. Coyle, "Women in the Clerical Occupations," *Annals of the American Academy of Political and Social Science* 143 (May 1929): 184.

15. William Henry Leffingwell, *Office Management: Principles and Practice* (Chicago and New York: A. W. Shaw, 1925), p. ix.

16. Ibid., p. 115.

17. W. H. Leffingwell, "What 'Scientific Management' Did for My Office," part 1 *System* 30 (1916): 618–19.

18. George F. Card, "Charting Each Stenographer's Work," *System* 23 (1913): 435–36.

19. R. H. Goodell, "Savings 42% on Routine Work," *System* 37 (1920): 1184.

20. Ibid., p. 1185.

21. Ibid.

22. Ibid.

23. Walter D. Fuller, "Standardization of Office Work," *Industrial Management* 53 (1917): 506–7.

24. J. W. Rowland, "5 People Do the Work of 11," *System* 39 (1921): 379.

25. R. N. Gooch, "More Letters—Lower Costs," *System* 24 (1913): 43.

26. W. H. Leffingwell, "This Plan More Than Doubled Our Typists' Output," *System* 30 (1916): 467. Emphasis in the original.

27. For those who are not familiar with the story of Schmidt, it is well worth reading. Frederick Winslow Taylor set it down in glowing detail in *The Principles of Scientific Management*, (New York: Norton, 1967 [1911]) pp. 41–47. It can also be found in Harry Braverman, *Labor and Monopoly Capital*, pp. 102–6.

28. William H. Leffingwell, "What 'Scientific Management' Did for My Office," part 2 *System* 31 (1917): 69–70.

29. Leffingwell, "This Plan More Than Doubled Our Typists' Output," pp. 463–64.

30. George A. Ricker, "How Much Is Your Stenographer Worth?" *System* 29 (1916): 215.

31. W. H. Leffingwell, "41 Ways to Save Time in an Office," *System* 31 (1917): 146.

32. Kendall Banning, "More Work and Fewer Mistakes," *System* 24 (1913): 397.

33. Homer S. Pace, "How We Doubled Our Output in Six Months," *System* 35 (1919): 634.

34. Ibid., p. 635.

35. Charles M. Ripley, "A Bundle of Office Ideas," *System* 36 (1919): 225.

36. Floyd W. Parsons, "Ways to Cut Business Costs," *World's Work* 45 (1923): 394. Parsons added that "in order to make sure that no employee wastes his time doing work that can be done by some other person receiving less pay, the manager had a slip printed and distributed, which read as follows: 'Many people are in the habit of saying that they can do a certain thing more quickly than they can tell someone else how to do it, and therefore many minor tasks are performed each day by various employees who could better devote their time to more important matters. Each worker should not forget that

though he may be able to do a certain job once in less time than it would take for a first explanation, it is nevertheless true that after a subordinate is taught, the high-priced time of the more important executive is saved over and over again.'" Ibid., p. 396.

37. William H. Leffingwell, "What 'Scientific Management' Did for My Office," part 1 *System* 30 (1916): 621. It is worth noting that Leffingwell assumed that the executive was a "he" and the memory clerk a "she." His assumption reflects the fact that not only were more executives men and many clerks women by this point, but also that scientific managers were concerned to fit the worker of the appropriate sex as well as skill to the job.

38. Parsons, "Ways to Cut Business Costs," p. 397.

39. Henry Anson Piper, "Cutting the Clerical Cost: Planning Procedure for Plant Offices in Large Organizations," *Industrial Management* 63 (1922): 121.

40. Banning, "More Work and Fewer Mistakes," p. 391.

41. Ibid., pp. 392–93.

42. C. S. Yoakum and Marion A. Bills, "Tests for Office Occupations," *Annals of the American Academy of Political and Social Science* 110 (November 1923): 73.

43. L. L. Thurstone, "A Standardized Test for Office Clerks," *Journal of Applied Psychology* 3 (1919): 248.

44. Eugene J. Benge, "Simple Tests for Selecting Office Workers: Making Sure, before Employing, That the Applicant Is Fitted for the Job," *Industrial Management* 61 (1921): 91.

45. Margaret P. Jaques, "Mental Tests for Typists and Stenographers," *Industrial Management* 58 (1919): 145.

46. "The use of tests in employment is as yet sufficiently unusual so that relatively few persons have come in contact with them. Some applicants may therefore be suspicious and even resentful when asked to take a test. These possible situations must be kept in mind and must be avoided so far as possible by tactful handling of subjects." Yoakum and Bills, "Tests for Office Occupations," p. 61.

47. G. W. Greenwood, "Simple Tests for Office Applicants," *Industrial Management* 57 (1919): 377. Emphasis in the original.

48. Leffingwell, "41 Ways to Save Time in an Office," pp. 139–40.

49. Ripley, "A Bundle of Office Ideas," p. 226.

50. Parsons, "Ways to Cut Business Costs," p. 395.

51. Goodell, "Saving 42% on Routine Work," p. 1184.

52. Pace, "How We Doubled Our Output in Six Months," p. 634. My emphasis.

53. This writer made no bones about who should be the boss in an office. Still on the subject of the flat-top desk, he stated that "there should be no locks except on the center drawer, in which can be kept the personal belongings of the user. The contents of the other drawers are the property of the company and should be open to the inspection of the department head at any time during the absence of the user of the desk." Wallace Clark, "Getting the Office Work Done—III: Furnishing and Equipping an Office," *Industrial Management* 60 (1920): 190.

54. Edward D. Page, "Handling Office Employees," *World's Work* 12 (1906): 7797.

55. From the experience of Adolph M. Schwarz, "An Artistic Office Cuts Our Payroll," *System* 42 (1922): 251–52.

56. Ripley, "A Bundle of Office Ideas," p. 226.

57. Stanley C. Tarrant, "How One Office Reduced Overtime Work," *System* 25 (1914): 658–59.

58. W. H. Leffingwell, "This Plan More Than Doubled Our Typists' Output," pp. 467–68.

59. Hinton Gilmore, "Gingering Up Office Work: Methods by Which the Office Manager of a Michigan Concern Obtained Better Work," *System* 28 (1915): 189.

60. Ibid., p. 185.

61. Ibid., p. 187. Gilmore also stated that "women, the office manager has found, are apt to respond to music in greater degree—so far as their attitude towards their work goes—than men; and he recommends music principally for offices where many girls are employed." Ibid.

62. Ibid., p. 189.

63. Ibid.

64. On this point, Harry Braverman sees the work of Frederick Winslow Taylor as the culmination rather than the beginning of changes in the organization of industrial production: "The publication of management manuals, the discussions of the problems of management, and the increasingly sophisticated approach taken in practice in the second half of the nineteenth century lend support to the conclusion of the historians of the scientific management movement that Taylor was the culmination of a pre-existing trend: 'What

Taylor did was not to invent something quite new, but to synthesize and present as a reasonably coherent whole ideas which had been germinating and gathering force in Great Britain and the United States throughout the nineteenth century. He gave to a disconnected series of initiatives and experiments a philosophy and a title.'" Lyndall Urwick and E. F. L. Brech, *The Making of Scientific Management*, 3 vols. (London, 1945–1948), 1: 17, quoted in Braverman, *Labor and Monopoly Capital*, p. 89.

65. Braverman, *Labor and Monopoly Capital*, pp. 72–73.

66. Goodell, "Saving 42% on Routine Work," p. 1184.

Chapter 7.

1. Frederick G. Nichols, *The Personal Secretary: Differentiating Duties and Essential Personal Traits* (Cambridge, Mass.: Harvard University Press, 1934), p. 30.

2. The word "secretary" derives from the Latin "secretarius," which referred to "a secretary, a notary, scribe, etc., a title applied to various confidential officers." "Secretarius," in turn, derived from "secretum," which meant "secret." An obsolete definition of "secretary" is "one who is entrusted with private or secret matters; a confident; one privy to a secret." The two most commonly used current definitions are (1) "one whose office it is to write for another; esp. one who is employed to conduct correspondence, to keep records, and (usually) to transact various other business, for another person or for a society, corporation, or public body"; and (2) "in the official designations of certain ministers presiding over executive departments of state" (*The Oxford English Dictionary*). "Secretary" often referred to someone whose duties went far beyond those of a stenographer or typist. Even today, a "secretary" can be an important executive or official, as in "secretary of the corporation" or "secretary of state." Formerly, the term for someone who wrote at the dictation of another was "amanuensis," derived from the Latin and meaning "one who copies or writes from the dictation of another." The word had fallen into disuse by the 1900s, being replaced by both "stenographer" and "secretary."

3. Ellen Lane Spencer, *The Efficient Secretary* (New York: Frederick A. Stokes, 1916), p. 4.

4. W. W. Charters and Isadore B. Whitley, *Analysis of Secretarial Duties and Traits* (Baltimore: Williams and Wilkins, 1924), pp. 177–78.

5. Edward Jones Kilduff, *The Private Secretary: The Duties and Opportunities of His Position*, rev. ed. (New York and London: Century, 1924), pp. 10–11. Also see Anne Pillsbury Anderson, "The Private Secretary," in Agnes F. Perkins, ed., *Vocations for the Trained Woman: Opportunities Other Than Teaching* (Boston: Women's Educational and Industrial Union, 1910), pp. 209–10. She argues that "in the majority of cases a stenographer grows into a secretary gradually, a busy man being only too thankful to throw into competent hands the details which are too vexatious and petty for his consideration."

6. Helen B. Gladwyn, "How I Became a Confidential Secretary" *Ladies' Home Journal* 33 (September 1916): 32.

7. Spencer, *The Efficient Secretary*, pp. 35–39.

8. Gladys Torson, "*Ask My Secretary . . .*": *The Art of Being a Successful Business Girl* (New York: Greenberg, 1940), p. 67. Torson went on to point out that "letters of congratulation and condolence seem to be harder for the average man to write than for the average woman, and you will do well to make a study of these two types of letters. They should be simple, not flowery, and above all they should sound sincere" (p. 68).

9. Edward Jones Kilduff, *The Private Secretary: His Duties and Opportunities* (New York: Century, 1917), p. 68. This is the first edition of a book that was revised in 1924. See note 5, above.

10. Ibid., p. 62.

11. Elizabeth Hilliard Ragan, "One Secretary as per Specifications," *Saturday Evening Post* 204 (12 December 1931): 10.

12. Kilduff, *The Private Secretary* (1917), p. 69.

13. Ibid., pp. 280–84. Gladys Torson also advised secretaries to seize the initiative in reforming their employers' "bad business habits," although she cautioned that "any measures you take will have to be diplomatic." Torson, "*Ask My Secretary*," p. 135.

14. Frances Avery Faunce, with Frederick G. Nichols, *Secretarial Efficiency* (New York and London: McGraw-Hill, 1939), p. 340.

15. Anderson, "The Private Secretary," p. 210.

16. Charters and Whitley, *Analysis of Secretarial Duties and Traits*, p. 30.

17. W. W. Charters and Isadore B. Whitley, *Summary of Report on*

Analysis of Secretarial Duties and Traits (New York: National Junior Personnel Service, 1924), p. 15. This book summarizes the larger volume by the same authors, *Analysis of Secretarial Duties and Traits* (see note 4, above). Another attempt at categorizing secretarial tasks was made by Frederick Nichols in *The Personal Secretary*; see tables 17 and 22.

18. Kilduff, *The Private Secretary* (1917), p. 89.

19. Ibid., pp. 210–11.

20. Faunce and Nichols, *Secretarial Efficiency*, p. 7. Emphasis in original.

21. Kilduff, *The Private Secretary* (1917), p. 145.

22. Ibid., p. 12.

23. Margaret A. Post, "Opportunities for Women in Secretarial Service," in Susan M. Kingsbury, ed., *Vocations for the Trained Woman: Agriculture, Social Service, Secretarial Service, Business of Real Estate*, published under the auspices of the Women's Educational and Industrial Union, Boston (New York: Longmans, Green, 1914), pp. 121–22.

24. Post, "Opportunities for Women in Secretarial Service," pp. 122–23. This study was based on the files of 1,500 "girls and women" who registered with the Women's Educational and Industrial Union in Boston for secretarial and stenographic work, and on reports of 371 women who had taken the secretarial course at Simmons College in Boston.

25. Torson, *"Ask My Secretary,"* pp. 62–63.

26. Kilduff, *The Private Secretary* (1917), p. 247.

27. Ibid., pp. 24, 31–32.

28. Gladys Torson, *How to Be a Hero to Your Secretary: A Handbook for Bosses*, (New York: Greenberg, 1941), pp. 46–47.

29. Lauretta Fancher, "His Secretary Speaking," *Colliers* 83 (13 April 1929): 40.

30. Federal Board for Vocational Education, *Commercial Occupations*, Opportunity Monograph No. 23 (1919). Cited in Elizabeth Kemper-Adams, *Women Professional Workers*, a study made for the Women's Educational and Industrial Union (New York: Macmillan, 1921), p. 228.

31. Kilduff, *The Private Secretary* (1917), p. 37.

32. Ibid., p. 52. Kilduff does not mention what should be done if the caller cannot be reached by phone and shows up for the appoint-

ment anyway. Presumably the good will of the caller would, in that case, be sacrificed to the employer's valuable time.

33. Ibid., pp. 194–95. My emphasis.

34. Frances Avery Faunce, "On the Adventure of Being a Secretary: Fourteen Tools of Secretarial Service," *Education* 55 (1935): 406. Emphasis in the original. Gladys Torson also remarked on the importance of the secretary as a buffer between her employer and his callers: "A secretary's first job is to keep things running smoothly for her employer. She must keep out pests, protect her employer from unnecessary interruptions . . ." Torson, "*Ask My Secretary*," p. 133.

35. Fancher, "His Secretary Speaking," p. 28.

36. Ibid.

37. Ibid.

38. Gladwyn, "How I Became a Confidential Secretary," p. 32.

39. Charters and Whitley, *Summary*, pp. 56, 60. The gift-buying aspect of a secretary's job was not necessarily a matter of common knowledge. One secretary told this story about her employer's wife: "She was telling me how wonderful her husband is. That he never forgets her birthday or their anniversary. She never has to hint about it like most wives. Well, I could have told her why. The first day I went to work for him, he gave me a list of all the anniversaries he has to remember and I marked them on my calendar. Then, when the time comes, I remind him, and he says, 'Oh, yes. Well, take a long noon hour and get something for me. About fifty dollars!' And I do. And have it wrapped and buy a card and put the pen in his hand and wait to be sure he writes, 'With much love from Jim.'" Fancher, "His Secretary Speaking," p. 40.

40. Mildred Harrington, "Too Much Dictation," *American Magazine* 110 (September 1930): 57, 137.

41. Fancher, "His Secretary Speaking," p. 28.

42. Harrington, "Too Much Dictation," p. 138.

43. Charters and Whitley, *Analysis of Secretarial Duties and Traits*, p. 136.

44. Charters and Whitley, *Summary*, pp. 49 and 59. In her list of "tools of secretarial service," Frances Avery Faunce included "passivity." "It is not easy to be passive while you are taking dictation, but your personality must not intrude on the scene. The employer is allowed the active mood at this point; the employed, the passive. If she can be passive on the outside and wholly alert on the inside, she is

being clever and efficient, and her employer is not the last one to recognize this." Faunce, "On the Adventure of Being a Secretary," p. 405.

45. Grace R. Hazard, "A Feather Duster: A Working Girl Looks at her Employers," *Scribner's Magazine* 85 (February 1929): 189. Emphasis in original.

46. Ibid., p. 194.

47. Torson, *"Ask My Secretary,"* p. 133. Torson went on to comment, "Until the Bolshevists take over, your boss's rights have precedence over yours. It is his privilege to give rein to his prima donna instincts if he feels like it, but it is not yours to do likewise. It is your privilege to resign, however, if the tantrums get too bad" (p. 134).

48. Ibid., p. 135. When Kilduff suggested that a secretary should get his employer to adopt systematic business habits, he was also careful to point out that "there is, of course, great need for tact and diplomacy in getting the employer to adopt a system." Kilduff, *The Private Secretary* (1917), p. 284.

49. Torson, *"Ask My Secretary,"* pp. 79–81.

50. Fancher, "His Secretary Speaking," p. 28.

51. Harrington, "Too Much Dictation," p. 57. Emphasis in original.

52. Faunce and Nichols, *Secretarial Efficiency*, pp. 17–18.

53. Gladwyn, "How I Became a Confidential Secretary," p. 32.

54. Charters and Whitley, *Analysis of Secretarial Duties and Traits*, p. 175. This is not in fact all that astonishing, if one considers that the most intelligent thing a secretary could do was to keep his or her job, and that "getting the employer's point of view" had a lot to do with keeping that job.

55. Charters and Whitley, *Summary*, pp. 59, 62.

56. Faunce and Nichols, *Secretarial Efficiency*, p. 54. My emphasis.

57. Kilduff, *The Private Secretary* (1917), p. 268.

58. Faunce and Nichols, *Secretarial Efficiency*, p. 517.

59. Sarah Louis Arnold, "The College Woman as Secretary," in Perkins, *Vocations for the Trained Woman: Opportunities Other Than Teaching*, p. 203.

60. Charters and Whitley, *Summary*, p. 60.

61. Ibid., p. 55.

62. Kilduff, *The Private Secretary* (1917), p. 270.

63. Torson, *"Ask My Secretary,"* p. 83.

64. Nichols, *The Personal Secretary*, p. 42.

65. Charters and Whitley, *Summary*, pp. 52–53.

66. Charters and Whitley, *Analysis of Secretarial Duties and Traits*, p. 53.

67. Charters and Whitley, *Summary*, pp. 54, 61. Out of the forty-seven traits that employers mentioned as being valuable in a secretary, "tact" held eighth place and "graciousness" twenty-first. Ibid., pp. 47–48.

68. Kilduff, *The Private Secretary* (1924), pp. 53–54. The original (1917) edition of this book did not even recognize the existence of female private secretaries. The second edition does, thus reflecting the transitional stage where an employer was as likely to have a female as a male private secretary.

69. Kilduff, *The Private Secretary* (1917), p. 273.

70. Spencer, *The Efficient Secretary*, p. 27.

71. Charters and Whitley, *Summary*, pp. 50, 54.

72. Ragan, "One Secretary as per Specifications," p. 10.

73. Anderson, "The Private Secretary," p. 209.

74. Ragan, "One Secretary as per Specifications," p. 11.

75. Harrington, "Too Much Dictation," p. 139.

76. Faunce and Nichols, *Secretarial Efficiency*, p. 10.

77. Torson, *"Ask My Secretary,"* pp. 39–40. Emphasis in the original.

78. Faunce, "On the Adventure of Being a Secretary," p. 405. Such exhortations to selflessness were common in the literature on how to be a good secretary.

79. One possible explanation for this state of affairs is that the line between private secretaries and other clerical workers was often fuzzy. In 1914 the author of "Opportunities for Women in Secretarial Service" states that "in this report the word 'secretary' is used throughout, though in many cases the individual is purely a stenographer, but by eliminating those receiving a weekly wage of less than $10—representing the lower grade of stenographic service—the higher grade stenographer may properly be included. The line between the two positions is so indistinct it does not seem feasible to attempt to make it hard and fast." Margaret A. Post, "Opportunities for Women in Secretarial Service," in Kingsbury, *Vocations for the Trained Woman*, p. 117. And for their survey of secretarial duties and traits, Charters and Whitley made "no direct attempt in getting the list of names to distinguish between secretaries and stenographers." Charters and Whitley, *Summary*, p. 14. Nonetheless, the very exis-

tence of books and articles that tried to distinguish the characteristics and tasks peculiar to private secretaries indicates that people were trying to make that fuzzy line more distinct.

80. Alba M. Edwards, *Comparative Occupation Statistics for the United States, 1870 to 1940*, part of the Sixteenth Census of the United States: 1940 (Washington, D.C.: Government Printing Office, 1943), p. 121.

81. The 1902 figure is from the *33rd Annual Report of the Massachusetts Bureau of Statistics of Labor,* Part IV: "Sex in Industry" (Boston: Wright and Potter, 1902), p. 148. There were 114 male private secretaries and 58 female. The 1926 figure is from the Massachusetts Department of Labor and Industries, "Salaries of Office Employees in Massachusetts," *Annual Report on the Statistics of Labor* (1926), Labor Bulletin no. 149. There were 33 male private secretaries and 172 female.

82. Alice Harriet Grady, "Training for Initiative in Secretarial Work," in Perkins, *Vocations for the Trained Woman*, p. 212.

83. Nichols, *The Personal Secretary*, pp. 82–83. My emphasis.

84. Kemper-Adams, *Women Professional Workers*, pp. 226–29.

Chapter 8.

1. Michel Crozier, for example, blames mechanization for the degradation of clerical work. Writing about office work in France, he states: "Mechanization and scientific organization have, it is true, completely transformed office work and even sales work. The introduction of accounting machines and then statistical machines has resulted in a series of small industrial revolutions, whose effects are now accelerated with the advent of automation. Since the introduction of these innovations, a split has taken place between highly qualified employees charged with handling matters demanding judgment, experience, and responsibility, and a mass of unskilled employees assigned a series of simple unchanging operations. In the administrative services of banks, insurance companies, or large accounting firms, there have for some time been numerous cases of assembly-line work, sometimes even using conveyor belts." Michel Crozier, *The World of the Office Worker*, trans. David Landau (Chicago: University of Chicago Press, 1971), p. 17.

Index